5

INGREDIENTS

ITALIAN

An Hachette UK Company
www.hachette.co.uk

First published in Great Britain in 2015 by
Hamlyn, a division of Octopus Publishing Group Ltd
Endeavour House
189 Shaftesbury Avenue
London
WC2H 8JY

Some of the recipes in this book have previously appeared in other books published
by Hamlyn.

ISBN 978-0-60062-919-1

A CIP catalogue record for this book is available from the British Library

Printed and bound in China

10 9 8 7 6 5 4 3 2

Commissioning Editor Eleanor Maxfield
Editor Pauline Bache
Designers Jeremy Tilston, Jaz Bahra & Eoghan O'Brien
Assistant Production Manager Caroline Alberti

Standard level spoon measurements are used in all recipes.
1 tablespoon = one 15 ml spoon
1 teaspoon = one 5 ml spoon

Both imperial and metric measurements have been given in all recipes. Use one set
of measurements only and not a mixture of both.

Eggs should be medium unless otherwise stated. The Department of Health advises
that eggs should not be consumed raw. This book contains dishes made with raw or
lightly cooked eggs. It is prudent for more vulnerable people such as pregnant and
nursing mothers, invalids, the elderly, babies and young children to avoid uncooked
or lightly cooked dishes made with eggs. Once prepared these dishes should be kept
refrigerated and used promptly.

Milk should be full fat unless otherwise stated.

Ovens should be preheated to the specific temperature – if using a fan-assisted
oven, follow manufacturer's instructions for adjusting the time and the temperature.

All microwave information is based on a 650-watt oven. Follow manufacturer's
instructions for an oven with a different wattage.

This book includes dishes made with nuts and nut derivatives. It is advisable for
customers with known allergic reactions to nuts and nut derivatives and those
who may be potentially vulnerable to these allergies, such as pregnant and nursing
mothers, invalids, the elderly, babies and children, to avoid dishes made with nuts
and nut oils. It is also prudent to check the labels of pre-prepared ingredients for
the possible inclusion of nut derivatives.

JUST 5 INGREDIENTS

CANCELLED

ITALIAN

**MAKE LIFE SIMPLE WITH MORE THAN 100 RECIPES
USING 5 INGREDIENTS OR FEWER**

hamlyn

Falkirk Council	
Askews & Holts	2016
641.55	£5.99

CONTENTS

INTRODUCTION

The recipes in this book have been chosen not only for their simplicity and great flavours, but also because they use just five or fewer main ingredients.

Applying a five-ingredient approach to cooking will help you create a repertoire of quick, easy adaptable dishes, that are not only cheap and tasty but that also require little shopping and preparation. You will learn to master some basic recipes in record time and learn to appreciate that cooking for yourself is a satisfying and empowering process.

This will make your life easier in three ways. First, because the recipes are straightforward there is less fiddly preparation, which will save you time. Second, you will find that shopping is simpler. How long do you really want to wander around a supermarket searching for something to cook? And third, it will save money. The five-ingredient approach will mean that you don't have a fridge full of half-used packets of strange ingredients, left over from previous meals that you will never use again.

Unlike other five-ingredient cookbooks, you won't have hundreds of hidden added extras to stock up on. This series requires you to remember 10 storecupboard extras only – simple, easy-to-remember basics you will no doubt already have to hand.

Start by stocking up on your storecupboard ten (see page 11). Make sure you have at least some of them at all times so that you know you are just five ingredients away from a decent meal.

Next, choose a recipe that suits the time you have to cook, your energy levels and your mood. Check what storecupboard ingredients you will need on the list. The five key ingredients you will need to buy and complete the dish are clearly numbered.

One of the best ways to eat cheaply is to avoid costly processed foods. Instead, buy basic ingredients such as vegetables, rice, pasta, fish and chicken, and build your meals around these. You should also try to avoid waste and not spend money on food you don't eat and that has to be thrown away. Buy food that lasts and plan around the lifetime dates of foods. If you have a freezer, freeze the leftovers for another day.

Plan your meals for the week so you need to go shopping only once a week. When you get into the habit of doing this the ingredients necessary for each meal will be waiting when you need them.

Buy in bulk to get the best prices. Make time to shop around and compare prices in the nearest supermarkets, online, your local shops and on market stalls to see which is cheapest. Stick to buying fruit and vegetables that are in season. Not only will they be better value than exotic produce flown in from abroad but you will be reducing your food miles. Finally, don't even think about spending precious cash on a supermarket's special offer unless it is something you will actually use. Three tins of pilchards in mustard sauce for the price of one is good value only if you are going to eat them.

Italian food is now so popular that classics such as lasagne or tiramisu have become household favourites in all corners of the world. Fuss-free homely food, fresh ingredients and simple techniques all make for a cuisine that has instant appeal to the modern cook.

Italians love their food so much that the dining table is the hub of the family. It is often argued that there is no such thing as Italian food but rather lots of regional culinary traditions. Fresh pasta, for instance, is a northern dish and is hardly ever eaten in southern Italy. In the south, cooks exclusively use olive oil, while in the first half of the 20th century butter was the cooking medium of choice in the north. The divisions used to be distinct: pizza, tomatoes, mozzarella cheese and chilli belonged to the south, while risotto, cream and black pepper were essentially northern. Today, the borders are blurred and favourite regional ingredients and dishes have become popular throughout the country and beyond. The recipes in this book represent family favourites from all over the country. Most are traditional, while some are inspired by contemporary flavour combinations.

The Italian cook depends on a well-stocked larder. Most of these ingredients are available in supermarkets, with only the more unusual ones requiring a trip to an Italian deli.

Anybody can cook Italian, and whether you are throwing together a quick pasta dish or letting a stew slowly simmer on the hob, the beauty of Italian cooking is that most dishes don't demand a lot of preparation time. For this reason, having a good repertoire of dishes to hand can be a lifesaver for busy weekday family meals and for entertaining alike. We've made some suggestions to get you started on the following pages.

WEEKLY PLANNER

SOMETHING TO CELEBRATE

MONDAY
Monkfish in Salsa D'Agrumi (see page 68)

TUESDAY
Veal Escalopes with Parma Ham (see page 98)

WEDNESDAY
Squid with Lemon & Caper Dressing (see page 58)

THURSDAY
Saffron Risotto (see page 140)

FRIDAY
Frozen Bellini (see page 178)

SATURDAY
Roast Poussins with Oregano (see page 110)

STORECUPBOARD 10

The only extras you will need!

1 Sugars
2 Flours
3 Oils & vinegars
4 Baking powder
5 Salt
6 Pepper
7 Stocks
8 Onion
9 Garlic
10 Lemon & lemon juice

SHOPPING LIST:

- 875 g (1¾ lb) monkfish tail
- 4 veal escalopes, about 150 g (5 oz) each
- 4 slices of Parma ham
- 8 small or 4 large squid
- 2 poussins, about 500 g (1 lb) each
- 1 leg of lamb, about 1.5 kg (3 lb), trimmed of excess fat
- 50 g (2 oz) salted anchovies
- 800 ml (1 pint 7 fl oz) dry white wine
- 2 tablespoons capers
- 300 g (10 oz) arborio, carnaroli or vialone nano rice
- 100 ml (3½ fl oz) sweet sparkling wine
- 3 oranges
- 750 g (1½ lb) ripe peaches
- 150 g (5 oz) peppery mixed salad leaves
- 2 tablespoons flat leaf parsley
- parsley sprigs
- 4 sage leaves
- 1 teaspoon ground cumin
- ½ teaspoon saffron threads
- 2 tablespoons oregano
- 10 juniper berries
- 4 rosemary sprigs
- 125 g (5 oz) butter
- Parmesan cheese

SUNDAY
Roast Lamb with Wine & Juniper (see page 96)

WEEKLY PLANNER

ON A BUDGET

MONDAY
Baked Cod with Tomatoes & Olives (see page 76)

TUESDAY
Baked Aubergines & Mozzarella (see page 136)

WEDNESDAY
Pork Chops with Lemon & Thyme (see page 108)

THURSDAY
Mussels Alla Marinara (see page 72)

FRIDAY
Tuna & Pesto Burgers (see page 78)

SATURDAY
Mozzarella & Tomato Ciabatta (see page 28)

STORECUPBOARD 10

The only extras you will need!

1   Sugars
2   Flours
3   Oils & vinegars
4   Baking powder
5   Salt
6   Pepper
7   Stocks
8   Onion
9   Garlic
10 Lemon & lemon juice

SHOPPING LIST:

- 4 cod fillets, about 175 g (6 oz) each
- 4 pork chops, about 200 g (7 oz) each
- 150 g (5 oz) prosciutto
- 4 fresh tuna steaks, about 175 g (6 oz) each
- 2 kg (4 lb) mussels, cleaned
- 100 g (3½ oz) pitted black olives
- 2 tablespoons capers in brine, drained
- 1 tablespoon tomato purée
- 250 g (8 oz) can chopped tomatoes
- 400 g (13 oz) can chopped tomatoes
- 150 ml (¼ pint) dry white wine
- 6 ciabatta rolls
- 4 mini pizza bases
- 4 tablespoons basil pesto
- 400 g (13 oz) cherry tomatoes
- 2 large or 2 small tomatoes
- 2 large tomatoes
- 2 aubergines
- 1 large or 2 small avocados
- 1 kg (2 lb) floury potatoes
- 50 g (2 oz) mixed salad leaves
- 50 g (2 oz) rocket leaves
- 1 small red chilli
- 8 thyme sprigs
- 25 g (1 oz) basil leaves
- 35 g (1¼ oz) parsley
- 550 g (1 lb 1½ oz) mozzarella cheese
- 200 ml (7 fl oz) double cream
- 50 g (2 oz) butter

SUNDAY
Quick Prosciutto & Rocket Pizza (see page 122)

5 FOR PASTA

Pasta is the classic Italian dish, and with just 5 key ingredients, these recipes provide endless variations on this fast, easy supper, all with only 5 ingredients.

Spinach & Gorgonzola Gnocchi (see page 132)

Red Pepper & Cheese Tortellini (see page 134)

Orechiette with Broccoli (see page 144)

King Prawn & Courgette Linguine (see page 88)

Fusilli with Tuna, Capers & Mint (see page 70)

5 FOR CLASSIC DISHES

Italian is the world's best-loved cuisine and these recipes showcase the classic flavours that have made it so popular all over the world, all with only 5 ingredients.

Carpaccio of Fresh Tuna (see page 26)

Olive, Onion & Rosemary Focaccia (see page 34)

Chicken Milanese (see page 92)

Spaghetti with Clams & Chilli (see page 64)

Pear & Almond Cake (see page 172)

5 FOR CHEESE-LOVERS

Adding a little extra indulgence to both sweet and savoury dishes, these cheesy treats provide delicious meals, with only 5 ingredients.

Mozzarella in Carrozza (see page 50)

Fusilli with Parmesan & Pine Nuts (see page 152)

Grilled Radicchio, Fontina & Speck (see page 104)

Baked Polenta with Gorgonzola (see page 146)

Lemon & Ricotta Tart (see page 182)

5 FOR A PACKED LUNCH

A packed lunch doesn't have to mean a sad sandwich every day, as these great 5-ingredient additions to any lunch box prove.

Tuna & Borlotti Bean Salad (see page 52)

Tomatoes Stuffed with Rice (see page 130)

Panzanella Salad (see page 44)

Spinach & Pea Frittata (see page 156)

Balsamic Figs with Parma Ham (see page 30)

5 FOR WARMING UP

Indulgent roasts, warming stews and comforting soups, with only 5 ingredients, these winter warmers will mean you'll be relaxing by the fire in no time.

Calves' Liver & Caramelized Onions (see page 94)

Caldo Verde (see page 36)

Pork Braised in Milk (see page 100)

Chestnut, Rice & Pancetta Soup (see page 112)

Veal with Wine & Lemon (see page 114)

5 FOR KIDS

Kids will love these tastes of Italian cooking, and with only 5 ingredients each, you'll love making them!

Tortilla Pizza with Salami (see page 118)

Roast Chicken with Herbs & Garlic (see page 102)

Ricotta & Red Onion Tortillas (see page 150)

Cherry Tomato & Rocket Pizza (see page 142)

Chocolate Sorbet (see page 174)

ANTIPASTI & BREADS

MAKES ABOUT 20 STICKS

Preparation time 20 minutes, plus 30 minutes proving
Cooking time 15 minutes

INGREDIENTS

1   1¼ teaspoons fast-action dried yeast

2   100 g (3½ oz) unsalted butter

3   small bunch of basil, leaves torn into pieces

STORECUPBOARD

200 ml (7 fl oz) water; 2 tablespoons olive oil; 1 teaspoon salt; 400 g (13 oz) strong white bread flour; 1 teaspoon caster sugar; 4 garlic cloves, finely chopped; coarse sea salt; black pepper

Buttered Garlic & Basil Sticks

■ If using a bread machine, lift out the pan and fit the blade. Put the yeast, measurement water, olive oil, salt, flour and sugar in the pan, following the order specified in the manual. Fit the pan into the machine and close the lid. Set to the dough program.

■ If making the dough by hand, put the flour, salt, sugar and yeast into a bowl. Add the oil and measurement water and mix with a wooden spoon until a rough dough forms. Use your hands to bring it together into a ball. Place it on a lightly floured work surface and knead for about 10 minutes until you have smooth, elastic dough.

■ At the end of the program or kneading process, turn the dough out on to a floured surface and cut it in half. Roll each half to a thin oval about 35 × 18 cm (14 × 7 in). Transfer to 2 greased baking sheets and cut into 2.5 cm (1 in) strips, making cuts a little in from the edge of the dough so the strips are still held together at the ends.

■ Sprinkle the dough with a little coarse salt. Cover loosely with oiled clingfilm and leave in a warm place for 30 minutes or until the dough has risen around the edges.

■ Bake in a preheated oven, 220°C (425°F), Gas Mark 7, for 8–10 minutes until the bread sounds hollow when tapped with the fingertips. Transfer to 2 large plates.

■ Melt a small piece of butter in a saucepan and fry the garlic for 2–3 minutes until beginning to brown. Add the remaining butter, the basil leaves and pepper to taste. When the butter has melted, brush this over the hot bread, separate into sticks and serve immediately, with your choice of dip.

SERVES 3

Preparation time 10 minutes
Cooking time 28 minutes

INGREDIENTS

1	18 thick asparagus spears, trimmed
2	250 g (8 oz) mozzarella cheese
3	250 g (8 oz) thinly sliced prosciutto
4	75 g (3 oz) butter, plus extra for greasing

STORECUPBOARD

black pepper

Asparagus & Prosciutto Wraps

■ Plunge the asparagus into a large saucepan of salted boiling water, then cook over a medium heat for 4–8 minutes, or until just tender.

■ Drain and plunge into cold water. When cooled, drain again and set aside.

■ Cut the mozzarella into 18 equal slices. Separate the prosciutto slices into 6 even piles and cut the butter into 12 even-sized knobs.

■ Take 3 asparagus spears and put them on 1 bundle of prosciutto. Put 2 pieces of mozzarella in between the spears, along with a knob of butter. Wrap the prosciutto around the asparagus, using all the slices in the pile. Repeat until you have 6 bundles.

■ Lightly grease an ovenproof dish and arrange the asparagus bundles over the base. Put a slice of mozzarella and a knob of butter on each bundle. Season with pepper and bake at the top of a preheated oven, 200°C (400°F), Gas Mark 6, for 20 minutes.

CREATE A SAUCE

For asparagus with lemon & garlic butter sauce, cook the asparagus spears as for the main recipe. Meanwhile, put 125 g (4 oz) butter, 1 crushed garlic clove, finely grated rind of 1 lemon and a little pepper in a saucepan and cook gently until the garlic is soft. Whisk in 1 tablespoon lemon juice and serve drizzled over the asparagus.

INGREDIENTS

1 250 g (8 oz) piece of tuna loin

2 1 tablespoon salted capers, rinsed

3 125 g (4 oz) wild rocket leaves

4 Parmesan cheese shavings, to serve

STORECUPBOARD

juice of 3 lemons; 150 ml (¼ pint) extra virgin olive oil; 1 garlic clove, finely chopped; salt and black pepper

Carpaccio of Fresh Tuna

■ Trim the tuna of any membrane or gristle. Wrap tightly in clingfilm and put in the freezer for about 1 hour until just frozen but not rock solid.

■ Meanwhile, whisk together the lemon juice, oil, garlic and capers in a bowl. Add salt and pepper to taste and whisk until emulsified.

■ Unwrap the tuna and thinly slice with a sharp, thin-bladed knife. Arrange the slices on 4 large serving plates. Spoon the dressing over the tuna. Top with a tangle of rocket leaves and scatter with Parmesan shavings.

CHANGE THE FISH

For fresh swordfish carpaccio, replace the tuna with a 250 g (8 oz) piece of swordfish. Freeze, thinly slice and arrange on plates as for the main recipe. Whisk together the lemon juice, olive oil and garlic, also adding 2 tablespoons chopped flat leaf parsley, instead of the capers. Spoon over the plated fish and top with the rocket. Omit the Parmesan cheese.

SERVES 2

Preparation time 5 minutes
Cooking time 12–13 minutes

INGREDIENTS

1 2 ciabatta rolls

2 50 g (2 oz) mozzarella cheese

3 2 large tomatoes

4 1 large or 2 small avocados

5 1 tablespoon roughly chopped basil

STORECUPBOARD

black pepper

Mozzarella & Tomato Ciabatta

■ Put the ciabatta rolls on a baking sheet and warm in a preheated oven, 180°C (350°F), Gas Mark 4, for about 10 minutes.

■ Meanwhile, thinly slice the mozzarella and slice the tomatoes. Halve, stone, peel and slice the avocados.

■ Remove the rolls from the oven and cut each roll in half. Layer the avocado, mozzarella and tomato slices on the 2 bottom halves, add the basil and sprinkle with pepper. Return the bottom halves with the filling to the oven for 2–3 minutes or until the mozzarella has melted. Put the top halves on top and serve immediately.

ADD PESTO & PEPPERS

For pesto, mozzarella & roasted pepper ciabatta, bake and halve 2 ciabatta rolls as for main recipe. Spread 1 teaspoon pesto over the bottom halves of each ciabatta, layer with the mozzarella and a few drained roasted peppers from a jar. Omit the avocado and tomato, add the basil and season. Cook in the oven as for the main recipe.

SERVES 4

Preparation time 5 minutes
Cooking time 4–5 minutes

INGREDIENTS

1   8 ripe fresh figs

2   12 slices of Parma ham

3   50 g (2 oz) wild rocket leaves

STORECUPBOARD

2 tablespoons balsamic vinegar; extra virgin olive oil, for drizzling; salt and black pepper

Balsamic Figs with Parma Ham

■ Cut the figs in half and arrange, cut-side up, on a baking sheet. Brush with the vinegar and lightly drizzle with oil. Season with a little salt and a generous grinding of pepper. Cook under a preheated high grill for 4–5 minutes until heated through and a little charred.

■ Arrange 3 slices of Parma ham on each serving plate. Top with the grilled figs and scatter with rocket leaves. Drizzle over a little more oil and serve while the figs are still warm.

TRY IT WITH FRESH MELON

For minted melon with Parma ham,
put a sliced small, ripe melon on
a platter with 12 slices of Parma
ham, then give this simple, classic
Italian antipasto a modern twist by
scattering it with 5 torn mint leaves
and drizzling over a little extra virgin
olive oil.

SERVES 4

Preparation time 15 minutes
Cooking time 10 minutes

INGREDIENTS

1 25 g (1 oz) wild rocket leaves

2 50 g (2 oz) fresh white breadcrumbs

3 1 kg (2 lb) mussels, cleaned

STORECUPBOARD

1 garlic clove; 4 tablespoons extra virgin olive oil;
salt and black pepper; lemon wedges, to serve

Rocket & Garlic Crumbed Mussels

■ Process the rocket and garlic in a food processor until roughly chopped. Add the breadcrumbs and pulse until combined, then stir in the oil. Season with salt and pepper. Cover and chill until needed.

■ Put the mussels in a large saucepan with a tight-fitting lid and add water to a depth of 2.5 cm (1 in). Cover and bring to the boil over a high heat. Cook the mussels, shaking the pan frequently, for 2–3 minutes, or until the shells have opened. Drain, discarding any that remain closed. Pull away and discard the empty shell halves, reserving only the halves with the mussels attached.

■ Place the mussels, flesh-side up, on a baking sheet. Divide the breadcrumb topping between the mussels and cook on the top shelf of a preheated high grill for 1–2 minutes until the breadcrumbs are golden. Serve immediately with lemon wedges on the side.

SERVES 6

Preparation time 20 minutes, plus 2 hours standing
Cooking time about 20 minutes

INGREDIENTS

1   **15 g (½ oz) fresh yeast or 1½ teaspoons fast-action dried yeast**

2   **50 g (2 oz) pitted black olives**

3   **3 rosemary sprigs**

STORECUPBOARD

large pinch caster sugar; 225 ml (7½ fl oz) lukewarm water; 50 g (11½ oz) Italian '00' flour or plain flour, plus extra for dusting; ½ teaspoon salt; olive oil, for oiling and drizzling; 1 onion, thinly sliced; coarse sea salt, for sprinkling

Olive, Onion & Rosemary Focaccia

■ Dissolve the yeast in a bowl with the sugar, measurement water and half the flour. Cover with a moist cloth and leave to stand in a warm place for 15 minutes until foamy.

■ Stir the salt into the remaining flour, then tip into the yeast mixture. Stir with one hand to form a moist dough. Knead on a floured work surface for 10 minutes until smooth and elastic. It should be very soft and slightly sticky. If too sticky to handle, add a little more flour. Put in an oiled bowl, cover with a moist cloth and leave to rise in a warm place for 1 hour, or until doubled in size.

■ Gently knead half the onion and olives into the dough. Transfer to a lightly oiled rectangular baking tray, about 20 × 30 cm (8 × 12 in), stretching it to fill the tray. Cover with a moist cloth and leave to rise in a warm place for 30 minutes. Make deep dimples on the surface with your finger. Scatter with the rosemary and remaining onion and olives and drizzle with oil. Cover again and leave to rise for 15 minutes.

■ Sprinkle the top of the focaccia with coarse sea salt. Bake in a preheated oven, 200°C (400°F), Gas Mark 6, for 20 minutes. Check if the bread is ready. If not, bake for a further 5 minutes. Turn out on to a wire rack and leave to cool. Eat warm or at room temperature on the same day.

SERVES 4

Preparation time 15 minutes
Cooking time 35-40 minutes

INGREDIENTS

1. 125 g (4 oz) dark green cabbage, e.g. Cavolo Nero

2. 625 g (1½ lb) floury potatoes, cut into small chunks

3. 400 g (13 oz) can cannellini beans, drained

4. 15 g (½ oz) fresh coriander, roughly chopped

STORECUPBOARD

4 tablespoons olive oil; 1 large onion, chopped; 2 garlic cloves, chopped; 1 litre (1¾ pints) vegetable stock; salt and black pepper

Caldo Verde

■ Discard any tough stalk ends from the cabbage and roll the leaves up tightly. Using a large knife, shred the cabbage as finely as possible.

■ Heat the oil in a large saucepan and gently fry the onion for 5 minutes. Add the potatoes and cook, stirring occasionally, for 10 minutes. Stir in the garlic and cook for a further 1 minute.

■ Add the stock and bring to the boil. Reduce the heat and simmer gently, covered, for about 10 minutes until the potatoes are tender. Use a potato masher to lightly mash the potatoes into the soup so that they are broken up but not completely puréed.

■ Stir in the beans, shredded cabbage and coriander and cook gently for a further 10 minutes. Season to taste with salt and pepper.

SERVES 4

Preparation time 10 minutes, plus standing
Cooking time 10 minutes

INGREDIENTS

1	250 g (8 oz) dried orzo
2	250 g (8 oz) frozen peas, defrosted
3	6 spring onions, roughly chopped
4	8 bottled marinated artichoke hearts, drained and thickly sliced
5	4 tablespoons chopped mint

STORECUPBOARD

5 tablespoons extra virgin olive oil; 2 garlic cloves, crushed; finely grated rind and juice of ½ unwaxed lemon, plus extra grated rind to garnish; salt and black pepper

Artichoke, Pea & Mint Salad

■ Cook the orzo in a large saucepan of salted boiling water according to the packet instructions until al dente, adding the peas to the pan 3 minutes before the end of the cooking time. Drain thoroughly.

■ Meanwhile, heat 2 tablespoons of the oil in a frying pan over a medium heat, add the spring onions and garlic and cook, stirring, for 1–2 minutes until softened.

■ Stir in the orzo and peas with the artichokes, mint and remaining oil. Toss well, season with salt and pepper, then leave to stand for 10 minutes. Stir in the lemon rind and juice and serve the salad warm, garnished with lemon rind.

MAKES 1 LARGE LOAF

Preparation time 20 minutes, plus 45 minutes proving
Cooking time 40 minutes

INGREDIENTS

1 2 tablespoons milk powder

2 2 teaspoons fennel seeds, lightly crushed

3 1 tablespoon chopped rosemary plus rosemary sprigs, to garnish

4 2 teaspoons fast-action dried yeast

5 100 g (3 oz) raisins

STORECUPBOARD

325 ml (11 fl oz) water; 100 ml (3½ fl oz) olive oil; 2 teaspoons sea salt, plus extra; 600 g (1 lb 3 oz) strong white bread flour; 1 tablespoon caster sugar

Olive Oil, Rosemary & Raisin Bread

■ If using a bread machine, lift out the pan and fit the blade. Put the ingredients, except the raisins and rosemary sprigs, in the pan, following the order specified in the manual. Add the seeds and rosemary with the flour. Fit the pan into the machine and close the lid. Set to the dough program, adding the raisins when the machine beeps.

■ If making the dough by hand, put the flour, milk powder, fennel seeds, chopped rosemary, salt, sugar and yeast into a bowl. Add the oil and measurement water and mix with a wooden spoon until a rough dough forms. Add the raisins, then use your hands to bring it together into a ball. Place it on a lightly floured work surface and knead for about 10 minutes until you have smooth, elastic dough.

■ At the end of the program or kneading process, turn the dough out on to a floured surface and shape it into a round. Make a hole through the centre of the loaf with your fingertips, then enlarge it with your hand until the dough is ring-shaped with a hole 10 cm (4 in) in diameter in the middle. Put the dough on a large, greased baking sheet, cover loosely with oiled clingfilm and leave to rise in a warm place for about 45 minutes or until it has almost doubled in size.

■ Score the dough at intervals with a floured knife and scatter with rosemary sprigs and sea salt. Bake in a preheated oven, 220°C (425°F), Gas Mark 7, for 40 minutes until risen and golden. Check the loaf after 20 minutes. If the rosemary sprigs are over-browning, replace them with fresh ones and cover the loaf with foil for the remainder of the baking time.

SERVES 4

Preparation time 15 minutes
Cooking time 10 minutes

INGREDIENTS

 1 kg (2 lb) squid, cleaned

STORECUPBOARD

vegetable oil, for deep-frying; 75 g (3 oz) plain flour; salt; lemon wedges, to serve

Fried Calamari

■ Cut the squid bodies into rings. Dry the rings and the tentacles thoroughly with kitchen paper.

■ Heat enough oil for deep-frying in a deep saucepan to 180–190°C (350–375°F), or until a cube of bread browns in 30 seconds. Season the squid with salt, then coat half in the flour, shaking off any excess. Add to the hot oil and cook for 2–3 minutes, or until golden and crisp. Remove with a slotted spoon and drain on kitchen paper. Scatter with a pinch of salt. Repeat with the remaining squid. Serve immediately with lemon wedges.

INGREDIENTS

| 1 | 600 g (1¼ lb) large tomatoes |

| 2 | 150 g (5 oz) ciabatta bread |

| 3 | handful of basil leaves, plus extra to garnish |

| 4 | 12 pickled white anchovies, drained |

STORECUPBOARD

1 tablespoon sea salt; ½ red onion, finely chopped; 1 tablespoon red wine vinegar; 2 tablespoons olive oil; salt and black pepper

Panzanella Salad

■ Roughly chop the tomatoes into 1.5 cm (¾ in) pieces and put them in a non-metallic bowl. Sprinkle over the sea salt and leave to stand for 1 hour.

■ Remove the crusts from the ciabatta and tear the bread into rough chunks.

■ Give the tomatoes a good squash with clean hands, then add the bread, onion, basil, vinegar and oil. Season to taste with salt and pepper. Mix together carefully and transfer to serving plates. Garnish with the drained anchovies and extra basil leaves and serve.

SERVES 6-8

Preparation time 10 minutes, plus cooling and chilling
Cooking time 1½ hours

INGREDIENTS

1	1 teaspoon whole cloves
2	500 g (1 lb) prepared octopus, bought at least 2 days before being cooked, and placed in the freezer for 48 hours to tenderize the meat
3	4 tablespoons chopped parsley

STORECUPBOARD

1 onion, cut into wedges; 2 litres (3½ pints) water; 6 tablespoons extra virgin olive oil; 2 garlic cloves, crushed; 1 teaspoon white wine vinegar; salt and black pepper

Octopus with Garlic Dressing

■ Put the onion, cloves and 1 tablespoon salt in a large saucepan and add the measurement water. Bring to the boil. Using tongs, dip the octopus in and out of the water about 4 times, returning the water to the boil before re-dipping, then immerse the octopus completely in the water. (This helps to make the flesh tender.) If there are several pieces of octopus, dip them 1 at a time.

■ Reduce the heat and cook the octopus very gently for 1 hour, then check to see whether it's tender. Cook for a further 15–30 minutes if necessary. Leave it to cool in the liquid, then drain, cut into bite-sized pieces and place a non-metallic bowl.

■ Mix the oil with the garlic, parsley, vinegar and add salt and pepper to taste, then add the whole mixture to the bowl. Mix well, cover and chill for several hours or overnight before serving.

SERVES 4

Preparation time 10 minutes
Cooking time 5 minutes

INGREDIENTS

1. 4 thick slices of country bread

2. 2 tablespoons chopped flat leaf parsley, plus extra to garnish

3. 4 small fresh Portobello mushrooms

STORECUPBOARD

2 garlic cloves, bruised; extra virgin olive oil, for drizzling; lemon juice, for drizzling; truffle oil, for drizzling; salt and black pepper

Portobello Bruschetta with Truffle Oil

■ Toast the bread slices on both sides under a preheated medium grill, in a preheated ridged griddle pan or over a barbecue. Rub 1 side of each toasted slice with the bruised garlic, then drizzle with the oil and sprinkle with the parsley.

■ Pick over the mushrooms and brush off any grit. Remove the stalks and thinly slice. Slice the caps as thinly as possible.

■ Cut the toasted slices in half. Scatter over the sliced mushroom stalks, drizzle with a little lemon juice and season with salt and pepper. Cover with the sliced mushroom caps. Drizzle with more lemon juice and a little truffle oil, season again with pepper and garnish with a little chopped parsley. Serve immediately.

ADD RADICCHIO

For Parmesan, Portobello mushroom & radicchio bruschetta, prepare the bruschetta as for the main recipe, omitting the parsley and lemon and dividing a handful of shredded radicchio leaves between each bread slice before adding the mushrooms. Top each bruschetta with a couple of Parmesan shavings, season with salt and pepper and drizzle with extra virgin olive oil instead of the truffle oil.

SERVES 4

Preparation time 10 minutes
Cooking time 15 minutes

INGREDIENTS

1   3 eggs, lightly beaten

2   3 tablespoons full-fat milk

3   200 g (7 oz) mozzarella cheese (drained weight), cut into 5 mm (¼ in) thick slices

4   8 slices of white bread

5   12 basil leaves

STORECUPBOARD

50 g (2 oz) plain flour; 4 tablespoons olive oil; salt and black pepper

Mozzarella in Carrozza

■ Combine the eggs and milk in a bowl and season lightly with salt and pepper. Put the flour in a separate bowl.

■ Divide the mozzarella slices between 4 bread slices and top each with 3 basil leaves. Lay a second bread slice on each to make 4 sandwiches. Press down firmly on each sandwich with the heel of your hand, then cut off and discard the crusts.

■ Heat half the oil in a large frying pan over a medium heat. Turn 2 of the sandwiches, 1 at a time, briefly in the flour to give a light coating, then dip in the egg mixture, making sure that they are well covered. Add to the pan and cook for 3–4 minutes on each side until golden and crisp. Remove and keep warm in a low oven while you cook the second batch of sandwiches in the remaining oil.

SERVES 4

Preparation time 15 minutes, plus marinating
Cooking time 3 minutes

INGREDIENTS

1   400 g (13 oz) can borlotti beans, drained and rinsed

2   1 red chilli, deseeded and finely chopped

3   2 celery sticks, thinly sliced

4   200 g (7 oz) can tuna in olive oil, drained and flaked

5   50 g (2 oz) wild rocket leaves

STORECUPBOARD

1 tablespoon water (optional); 2 tablespoons extra virgin olive oil; 2 garlic cloves, crushed; ½ red onion, cut into thin wedges; finely grated rind and juice of 1 lemon; salt and black pepper

Tuna & Borlotti Bean Salad

■ Heat the borlotti beans in a saucepan over a medium heat for 3 minutes, adding the measurement water if starting to stick to the base.

■ Put the oil, garlic and chilli in a large bowl. Stir in the celery, onion and hot beans and season with salt and pepper. Cover and leave to marinate at room temperature for at least 30 minutes and up to 4 hours.

■ Stir in the tuna and lemon rind and juice. Gently toss in the rocket leaves, taste and adjust the seasoning with extra salt, pepper and lemon juice, if necessary.

MAKES 1 ROUND LOAF

Preparation time 25 minutes, plus 30 minutes proving
Cooking time 35 minutes

INGREDIENTS

1 1½ teaspoons fast-action dried yeast

2 3 teaspoons black olive pesto or sun-dried tomato pesto

3 50 g (2 oz) sun-dried tomatoes, drained and sliced

4 small bunch of basil

STORECUPBOARD

275 ml (9 fl oz) water; 7 tablespoons olive oil; 1 teaspoon salt; 475 g (15 oz) strong white bread flour; 2 teaspoons caster sugar; 1 large red onion, thinly sliced; 2 garlic cloves, finely chopped; 1 teaspoon caster sugar; coarse salt flakes

Onion & Tomato Schiacciata

■ If using a bread machine, lift out the pan and fit the blade. Put the yeast, measurement water, 3 tablespoons of the olive oil, salt, flour and sugar in the pan, following the order specified in the manual. Fit the pan and close the lid. Set to the dough program.

■ If making the dough by hand, put the flour, 1 teaspoon salt, 2 teaspoons sugar and yeast into a bowl. Add the measurement water and 3 tablespoons olive oil, mix with a wooden spoon until a rough dough ball forms. Knead on a lightly floured surface until you have a smooth, elastic dough (about 10 minutes).

■ Heat 1 tablespoon of the remaining oil in a frying pan. Add the onion and garlic and fry gently for 5 minutes until softened. Scoop out one-quarter and reserve for the topping. Add the remaining teaspoon of sugar to the onions left in the pan and cook for a few minutes more until caramelized.

■ At the end of the program or kneading process, turn the dough out on to a floured surface and cut it in half. Roll one half to a 23 cm (9 in) round. Place on an oiled baking sheet. Spread with the pesto. Top with the caramelized onions, three-quarters of the sun-dried tomatoes, half the basil leaves and drizzle with 2 tablespoons oil.

■ Roll out the remaining dough to a circle and cover the first circle. Sprinkle with the remaining onions, tomatoes, basil leaves and some coarse salt. Cover loosely with oiled clingfilm and leave to rise in a warm place for 30 minutes.

■ Bake in a preheated oven, 200°C (400°F), Gas Mark 6, for 25 minutes until golden brown and the centre is cooked through. Transfer to a chopping board, drizzle with the remaining oil and serve warm, cut into wedges.

FISH & SEAFOOD

Preparation time 10 minutes, plus marinating
Cooking time 5 minutes

INGREDIENTS

1 8 small or 4 large squid, cleaned and halved lengthways, tentacles discarded

2 1 teaspoon ground cumin

3 50 ml (2 fl oz) white wine

4 2 tablespoons capers

STORECUPBOARD

2 tablespoons olive oil; grated rind and juice of 1 lemon; salt and black pepper

Squid with Lemon & Caper Dressing

■ Open the squid out and pat dry with kitchen paper.

■ Lay them on a chopping board, shiny-side down and, using a sharp knife, lightly score a fine diamond pattern on the flesh, being careful not to cut all the way through. Place the squid in a non-metallic bowl along with the oil, cumin, lemon rind, half the lemon juice and a little pepper (no salt at this stage). Leave in the refrigerator to marinate for at least 30 minutes, but better still overnight.

■ Heat a frying pan until it is very hot. Add the squid to the pan in batches, scored-side down, and cook each batch for about 1–2 minutes, or until it turns white and loses its transparency. Remove from the pan and keep warm while cooking the rest of the squid.

■ Return the pan to the heat and deglaze the pan with the wine. Allow the wine to boil for a minute to burn off the alcohol. Remove the pan from the heat and add the remaining lemon juice and finally the capers. Season the squid with salt and pepper and serve with the pan juices poured over.

SERVES 4

Preparation time 10 minutes
Cooking time 15–20 minutes

INGREDIENTS

1	500 g (1 lb) small new potatoes, scrubbed
2	4 fresh tuna steaks, about 175 g (6 oz) each
3	100 g (3½ oz) baby spinach leaves, roughly chopped
4	griddled lime wedges, to serve

STORECUPBOARD

4 tablespoons olive oil; 2 tablespoons balsamic vinegar; salt and black pepper

Griddled Tuna Salad

■ Place the new potatoes in a steamer over boiling water and cook for 15 minutes or until tender.

■ Meanwhile, heat a griddle pan. Pat the tuna fillets dry with kitchen paper and cook in the pan for 3 minutes on each side for rare, 5 minutes for medium or 8 minutes for well done.

■ Remove the potatoes from the steamer. Slice them in half and place in a bowl. Add the spinach, olive oil and balsamic vinegar. Toss and season to taste. Divide the salad between 4 plates and serve with a slice of tuna arranged on the top of each, and a griddled lime wedge for squeezing.

SERVES 4

Preparation time 10 minutes
Cooking time 10 minutes

INGREDIENTS

1 4 trout fillets, about 200 g (7 oz) each

2 large handful of basil, roughly chopped, plus extra to garnish

3 50 g (2 oz) Parmesan cheese, freshly grated

4 salad, to serve

STORECUPBOARD

4 tablespoons olive oil, plus extra for greasing; 1 garlic clove, crushed; salt and black pepper

Trout with Pesto

■ Brush a baking sheet lightly with oil and place under a preheated very hot grill to heat up.

■ Put the trout fillets on to the hot sheet, sprinkle with salt and pepper and place under the grill for 8–10 minutes until lightly browned and the fish flakes easily when pressed with a knife.

■ Meanwhile, put the basil and garlic into a bowl. Work in the oil using a hand-held blender. Stir in the Parmesan cheese.

■ Remove the fish from the grill, transfer to serving plates, drizzle with the pesto, sprinkle with extra basil leaves to garnish and serve with salad.

SERVES 4

Preparation time 10 minutes
Cooking time 20 minutes

INGREDIENTS

1 ¼ teaspoon crushed dried chillies

2 400 g (13 oz) dried spaghetti

3 150 ml (¼ pint) dry white wine

4 1 kg (2 lb) clams, cleaned

5 2 tablespoons roughly chopped flat leaf parsley

STORECUPBOARD

5 tablespoons extra virgin olive oil; 2 garlic cloves, thinly sliced

Spaghetti with Clams & Chilli

■ Heat the oil in the largest frying pan you have or a wok over a low heat. Add the garlic and crushed chillies and leave to infuse for 6–8 minutes. If the garlic begins to colour, remove the pan from the heat and leave to infuse in the heat of the pan.

■ Cook the pasta in a large saucepan of salted boiling water for 8–10 minutes, or according to the packet instructions, until al dente, then drain.

■ Meanwhile, increase the heat under the frying pan and pour in the wine. Boil for 1 minute, then add the clams and cook, stirring, for 4–5 minutes until the shells have opened. Stir in the drained pasta and the parsley and toss over a high heat for 30 seconds. Serve immediately.

SERVES 2

Preparation time 10 minutes
Cooking time 25 minutes

INGREDIENTS

1   2 Dover sole, about 400 g (13 oz) each, skinned (ask your fishmonger to do this for you)

2   100 ml (3½ fl oz) dry white wine

3   200 ml (7 fl oz) passata

4   ½ teaspoon dried oregano

5   2 tablespoons capers in brine, rinsed

STORECUPBOARD

4 tablespoons olive oil; 1 garlic clove, roughly chopped; 50 g (2 oz) plain flour, seasoned with salt; pinch of caster sugar; salt and black pepper (optional)

Sole with Tomatoes & Capers

■ Heat the oil in a large frying pan over a low heat. Add the garlic and cook for 10 minutes. Discard the garlic and increase the heat to high.

■ Pat the sole dry with kitchen paper, then turn in the seasoned flour to coat both sides. Gently lower into the hot oil and cook for 4–5 minutes on each side until golden (if your pan isn't large enough, cook individually and keep the cooked sole warm in a low oven while you cook the remaining fish). Remove to a warmed serving plate.

■ Pour the wine into the frying pan and cook, stirring well with a wooden spoon to loosen any sediment from the base of the pan, for 1 minute. Add the passata, sugar, oregano and capers and bring to the boil.

Check the seasoning and add salt and pepper if necessary, then spoon the sauce over the fish. Serve immediately.

TRY A DIFFERENT SAUCE

For sole with lemon, parsley & garlic, cook the sole as for the main recipe and keep warm. Melt 50 g (2 oz) butter in the frying pan over a medium heat and stir in the grated rind of 1 lemon and 2 crushed garlic cloves. Cook for 2 minutes, then remove from the heat and stir in the juice of 1 lemon and 2 tablespoons finely chopped flat leaf parsley. Spoon over the fish and serve immediately.

SERVES 4

Preparation time 20 minutes
Cooking time 15 minutes

INGREDIENTS

1 875 g (1¾ lb) monkfish tail

2 finely grated rind and juice of 1 orange, pared orange rind and orange wedges

3 150 ml (¼ pint) dry white wine

4 2 tablespoons chopped flat leaf parsley and parsley sprigs

STORECUPBOARD

plain flour, seasoned with salt and black pepper, for coating; 2 tablespoons olive oil; finely grated rind and juice of 1 lemon; salt and black pepper; lemon wedges

Monkfish in Salsa D'Agrumi

■ Trim any membrane and dark meat from the monkfish. Remove the central bone by slitting the fish down the centre until you reach the bone. Turn the fish over and do the same on the other side. Ease out the bone, gently scraping the flesh away with the tip of a knife. Cut the fish into large chunks, then toss in seasoned flour to coat all over, shaking off the excess.

■ Heat the oil in a nonstick frying pan over a medium-high heat. Add the fish and cook until golden all over. Remove to a plate.

■ Add the grated orange and lemon rind and juice to the pan with the wine and boil rapidly. Reduce the heat, return the fish to the pan and simmer gently for 3–4 minutes, or until the fish is cooked through. Stir in the parsley and salt and pepper to taste.

■ Lift the fish out on to a warmed serving dish. Boil the sauce to reduce it a little more, then pour over the fish. Serve immediately, garnished with orange rind, parsley sprigs and orange and lemon wedges.

A SOLE ALTERNATIVE

For sole in lemon & basil sauce, dust
2 × 400 g (13 oz) skinned Dover
sole in seasoned plain flour and fry
in the oil, instead of the monkfish,
for 2 minutes on each side, until
golden. Remove to a plate then
continue as for the main recipe,
omitting the orange juice and rind
and adding 5 torn basil leaves to the
sauce instead of the parsley.

SERVES 4

Preparation time 10 minutes
Cooking time 12 minutes

INGREDIENTS

1 300 g (10 oz) canned tuna in olive oil

2 2 tablespoons capers in brine, drained and rinsed

3 ½ red chilli, deseeded and finely chopped

4 2 tablespoons roughly chopped mint

5 400 g (13 oz) dried fusilli

STORECUPBOARD

4 tablespoons extra virgin olive oil, plus extra for drizzling; finely grated rind of 1 lemon; 2 garlic cloves, crushed; salt

Fusilli with Tuna, Capers & Mint

■ Put the tuna with its oil in a large serving bowl. Break it up with a fork, then stir in the remaining ingredients, except for the pasta. Season with salt. Cover and leave to infuse while you cook the pasta.

■ Cook the pasta in a large saucepan of salted boiling water for about 10–12 minutes, or according to the packet instructions, until al dente.

■ Drain the pasta and toss into the sauce. Serve immediately with a bottle of extra virgin olive oil for anyone to drizzle a little extra over their serving.

Preparation time 15 minutes
Cooking time 15 minutes

INGREDIENTS

1   150 ml (¼ pint) dry white wine

2   400 g (13 oz) can chopped tomatoes

3   1 small red chilli, deseeded and finely chopped

4   2 tablespoons chopped flat leaf parsley, plus extra whole leaves to garnish

5   2 kg (4 lb) mussels, cleaned

STORECUPBOARD

3 tablespoons olive oil; 4 garlic cloves, chopped; salt and black pepper

Mussels Alla Marinara

■ Heat the oil in a large saucepan over a low heat. Add the garlic and cook for about 5 minutes until golden. Add the wine, tomatoes, chilli and chopped parsley and bring to the boil. Season well with salt and pepper.

■ Add the mussels to the pan, cover and cook over a high heat, shaking the pan frequently, for 4–5 minutes, or until the shells have opened. Stir well and discard any that remain closed.

■ Scatter the whole parsley leaves over the mussels and serve immediately.

SERVES 6

Preparation time 25 minutes, plus steaming and marinating
Cooking time 15 minutes

INGREDIENTS

1	6 red, orange or yellow peppers
2	12 artichoke hearts in olive oil, drained
3	24 anchovy fillets in olive oil, drained
4	1 tablespoon chopped oregano
5	2 hard-boiled eggs, finely chopped

STORECUPBOARD

2 garlic cloves, sliced; extra virgin olive oil, for drizzling; salt and black pepper

Stuffed Peppers

◾ Put the whole peppers in a grill pan and cook under a preheated high grill or over a barbecue until the skins begin to char. Turn the peppers and continue to cook until charred all over.

◾ Transfer the peppers to a plastic bag, seal and leave to steam for 10 minutes. Peel off the skins, then cut the peppers in half lengthways through the stalks and remove and discard the cores and seeds. Arrange the peppers, cut-side up, in a shallow dish.

◾ Cut the artichokes in half and put 2 halves in each pepper half. Lay 2 anchovy fillets over the artichokes. Season well with salt and pepper. Scatter over the garlic and oregano, then drizzle with oil.

◾ Cover and leave to marinate in the refrigerator overnight. Serve at room temperature, sprinkled with the chopped hard-boiled eggs.

SERVES 4

Preparation time 5 minutes
Cooking time 15 minutes

INGREDIENTS

| 1 | 250 g (8 oz) cherry tomatoes, halved |

| 2 | 100 g (3½ oz) pitted black olives |

| 3 | 2 tablespoons capers in brine, drained |

| 4 | 4 thyme sprigs, plus extra for garnish |

| 5 | 4 cod fillets, about 175 g (6 oz) each |

STORECUPBOARD

2 tablespoons extra virgin olive oil; 2 tablespoons balsamic vinegar; salt and black pepper

Baked Cod with Tomatoes & Olives

■ Combine the tomatoes, olives, capers and thyme sprigs in a roasting tin. Nestle the cod fillets in the pan, drizzle over the oil and balsamic vinegar and season to taste with salt and pepper.

■ Bake in a preheated oven, 200°C (400°F), Gas Mark 6, for 15 minutes.

■ Transfer the fish, tomatoes and olives to warmed plates. Spoon the pan juices over the fish and serve immediately.

TRY STEAMING

For steamed cod with lemon, arrange a cod fillet on each of 4 × 30 cm (12 in) squares of foil. Top each with ½ teaspoon grated lemon rind, a squeeze of lemon juice, 1 tablespoon extra virgin olive oil and salt and pepper to taste. Seal the edges of the foil together to form parcels, transfer to a baking sheet and cook in a preheated oven, 200°C (400°F), Gas Mark 6, for 15 minutes. Remove and leave to rest for 5 minutes. Open the parcels and serve sprinkled with chopped parsley.

Preparation time 5 minutes
Cooking time 4–6 minutes

INGREDIENTS

1	4 ciabatta rolls
2	4 fresh tuna steaks, about 175 g (6 oz) each
3	2 tomatoes, sliced
4	4 tablespoons basil pesto
5	50 g (2 oz) mixed salad leaves

STORECUPBOARD

1 tablespoon extra virgin olive oil, plus extra to drizzle; 1 lemon, halved; salt and black pepper

Tuna & Pesto Burgers

■ Heat a ridged griddle pan until hot. Split the rolls in half, add to pan and cook for 1-2 minutes on each side until lightly charred. Transfer to serving plates.

■ Brush the tuna steaks lightly with the oil and season with salt and pepper. Add to the pan and cook for 1 minute on each side.

■ Transfer each tuna steak to the base of a roll and squeeze over a little lemon juice from the lemon halves. Divide the tomato slices, pesto and salad leaves between the roll bases and drizzle over a little extra oil. Replace the roll tops and serve immediately.

SERVES 4

Preparation time 10 minutes
Cooking time 25 minutes

INGREDIENTS

1   300 g (10 oz) risotto rice

2   150 ml (¼ pint) dry white wine

3   125 g (4 oz) cream cheese

4   125 g (4 oz) smoked salmon, chopped

5   4 tablespoons chopped herbs (such as chives, parsley or dill)

STORECUPBOARD

2 teaspoons olive oil; 1 onion, finely chopped; 2 garlic cloves, crushed; 900 ml (1½ pints) simmering vegetable stock; salt and black pepper

Smoked Salmon Risotto

■ Heat the oil in a large saucepan, add the onion and garlic and fry for 2–3 minutes until they begin to soften.

■ Stir in the rice and continue to cook for 1 minute. Add the wine and cook, stirring, until all the wine has been absorbed.

■ Reduce the heat and add the stock a little at a time, stirring continuously, and allowing each amount of stock to be absorbed before adding the next. Continue until all the stock has been absorbed.

■ Stir in the cream cheese, smoked salmon and herbs, season to taste with salt and pepper and serve.

SERVES 4

Preparation time 10 minutes
Cooking time 3 minutes

INGREDIENTS

1 250 g (8 oz) strawberries, hulled

2 12 king scallops, without corals, cut into 3 slices

3 3 leeks, cut into matchstick-thin strips

4 250 g (8 oz) mixed salad leaves

5 20 strawberries, sliced

STORECUPBOARD

2 tablespoons balsamic vinegar; 1 tablespoon lemon juice, plus juice of 1 lemon; 50 ml (2 fl oz) olive oil; salt and black pepper; 1 tablespoon olive oil

Warm Scallop Salad

■ Put the 250 g (8 oz) strawberries, vinegar, lemon juice and 50 ml (2 fl oz) oil in a food processor or blender and process until smooth. Pass through a fine sieve or muslin cloth to remove the pips and set aside.

■ Season the scallops with salt and pepper and the remaining lemon juice.

■ Prepare the garnish. Heat 1 tablespoon oil in a nonstick frying pan, add the leeks and cook over a high heat, stirring, for 1 minute, or until golden brown. Remove and set aside.

■ Add the scallop slices to the pan and cook for 20–30 seconds on each side. Divide the salad leaves into quarters and pile in the centre of individual serving plates. Arrange the scallop slices over the salad.

■ Heat the strawberry mixture gently in a small saucepan for 20–30 seconds, then pour over the scallops and salad leaves. Scatter over the leeks and garnish with the strawberries. Sprinkle with a little pepper and serve.

Preparation time 5 minutes
Cooking time 8 minutes

INGREDIENTS

1 4 red snapper fillets, about 175 g (6 oz) each

2 250 g (8 oz) baby leaf spinach

3 1 teaspoon pumpkin seeds

4 1 teaspoon sunflower seeds

5 1 bunch of spring onions, shredded, to garnish

STORECUPBOARD

2 teaspoons olive oil

Griddled Red Snapper with Spinach

■ Heat a griddle pan over a medium heat, add the snapper fillets and cook for 4 minutes on each side or until cooked through and the fish flakes easily when pressed with a fork.

■ Meanwhile, steam the spinach until just tender. Drain well, then mix the pumpkin seeds, sunflower seeds and oil with the spinach in a bowl. Serve immediately with the snapper fillets on top, garnished with the shredded spring onions.

SERVES 4

Preparation time 10 minutes, plus infusing
Cooking time 20 minutes

INGREDIENTS

1 300 g (10 oz) ready-prepared squid, cleaned

2 12 raw prawns, unpeeled

3 12 live clams, cleaned

4 12 live mussels, scrubbed and debearded

5 2 tablespoons chopped parsley

STORECUPBOARD

2 garlic cloves, peeled and bruised; 6 tablespoons extra virgin olive oil; lemon wedges, to serve

Mixed Seafood Grill

■ Cut down the side of the squid so that it can be laid flat on a chopping board. Using a sharp knife, cut off the tentacles then lightly score the inside flesh in a crisscross pattern, then cut the squid into 3 cm (1¼ in) squares. Chill until required.

■ Make the dressing. Put the garlic in a small bowl, add the oil and stir in the parsley. Leave the flavours to infuse for at least 15 minutes.

■ When ready to serve, heat a ridged griddle pan over a high heat until searing hot. Lightly brush the prawns and squid with half the dressing. Add the prawns to the pan and cook for 3–4 minutes on each side or until they turn pink. Transfer to a warmed serving platter.

■ Add the squid flesh (but not the tentacles), the clams and mussels to the pan (discarding any that don't shut when tapped), and cook for 5–7 minutes or until the squid turns white and is charred and the clams and mussels have opened. Discard any that remain closed. Add the squid tentacles and cook for 2–3 minutes more, then transfer everthing to the serving platter and drizzle all the seafood with the remaining dressing. Serve immediately with lemon wedges.

SERVES 4

Preparation time 10 minutes
Cooking time 10–12 minutes

INGREDIENTS

1	400 g (13 oz) dried linguine
2	200 g (7 oz) peeled raw king prawns
3	1 fresh red chilli, deseeded and finely chopped
4	400 g (13 oz) courgettes, coarsely grated
5	50 g (2 oz) unsalted butter, cut into cubes

STORECUPBOARD

3 tablespoons olive oil; 2 garlic cloves, crushed; finely grated rind of 1 unwaxed lemon; salt

King Prawn & Courgette Linguine

■ Cook the pasta in a large saucepan of salted boiling water according to the packet instructions until al dente. Drain.

■ Meanwhile, heat the oil in a large frying pan over a high heat until the surface of the oil seems to shimmer slightly. Add the prawns, garlic, lemon rind and chilli, season with salt and cook, stirring, for 2 minutes until the prawns turn pink. Add the courgettes and butter, season with a little more salt and stir well. Cook, stirring, for 30 seconds.

■ Toss in the pasta and stir until the butter has melted and all the ingredients are well combined. Serve immediately.

TRY A PUMPKIN PASTA SAUCE

For squid & pumpkin sauce,
replace the prawns with 200 g
(7 oz) prepared squid rings and
the courgette with 400 g (13 oz)
coarsely grated pumpkin, and cook
as described in the main recipe.

MEAT &
POULTRY

SERVES 4

Preparation time 20 minutes
Cooking time 10–25 minutes

INGREDIENTS

1   4 boneless chicken breasts, about 150–175 g (5–6 oz) each, skinned

2   2 eggs, beaten

3   200 g (7 oz) dry white breadcrumbs

4   3 tablespoons flat leaf parsley, chopped

STORECUPBOARD

100 g (3½ oz) plain flour; 5 tablespoons olive oil; salt and black pepper; lemon wedges, to serve

Chicken Milanese

■ Lay the chicken breasts between 2 sheets of clingfilm and beat with a rolling pin until no more than 1 cm (½ in) thick.

■ Put the flour, eggs and breadcrumbs in 3 separate dishes and season the flour and eggs with salt and pepper. Stir the chopped parsley into the breadcrumbs. Turn each chicken breast in the flour, then dip into the eggs and coat in the breadcrumbs.

■ Heat the oil in a frying pan over a high heat. Add the flattened chicken breasts, 1 or 2 at a time, and cook for 2–3 minutes on each side until golden. Remove with a slotted spoon and drain on kitchen paper. Serve with lemon wedges.

SERVES 4

Preparation time 10 minutes
Cooking time 40–45 minutes

INGREDIENTS

1 50 g (2 oz) butter

2 625 g (1¼ lb) calves' liver, thinly sliced (ask your butcher to slice as thinly as possible)

3 2 tablespoons finely chopped flat leaf parsley

STORECUPBOARD

2 tablespoons olive oil; 2 large onions, thinly sliced; salt and black pepper

Calves' Liver & Caramelized Onions

■ Melt half the butter with the oil in a large frying pan with a tight-fitting lid. Add the onions and season with salt and pepper, then cover and cook over a very low heat, stirring occasionally, for 35–40 minutes until very soft and golden. Remove to a bowl and increase the heat under the pan to high.

■ Season the liver with salt and pepper and melt the remaining butter in the pan. Once the butter starts foaming, add the liver and cook for 1–2 minutes until browned. Turn over and return the onions to the pan. Cook for a further minute, then serve immediately with the parsley scattered over.

USE CHICKEN LIVER

For chicken liver & caramelized onions, cook the onions as for the main recipe and remove from the pan. Replace the calves' liver with 400 g (13 oz) chicken livers, coated in seasoned flour. Cook the livers in the remaining butter in the pan as for the main recipe for 4–5 minutes, turning once. Add 1 tablespoon aged balsamic vinegar, swirl in the pan for a couple of seconds, then return the caramelized onions to the pan. Cook for a further minute, stir in the parsley as for the main recipe and serve immediately.

SERVES 6

Preparation time 20 minutes
Cooking time 1 hour 35 minutes

INGREDIENTS

1 1 leg of lamb, about 1.5 kg (3 lb), trimmed of excess fat

2 10 juniper berries, crushed

3 50 g (2 oz) salted anchovies, boned and rinsed

4 1 tablespoon chopped rosemary plus 2 rosemary sprigs

5 300 ml (½ pint) dry white wine

STORECUPBOARD

2 tablespoons olive oil; 3 garlic cloves, crushed; 2 tablespoons balsamic vinegar; salt and black pepper

Roast Lamb with Wine & Juniper

■ Heat the oil in a roasting tin in which the lamb will fit snugly. Add the lamb and cook until browned all over. Leave to cool.

■ Pound 6 of the juniper berries, the garlic, anchovies and chopped rosemary with a pestle and mortar. Stir in the vinegar and mix to a paste. Make small incisions all over the lamb with a small, sharp knife. Spread the paste over the lamb, working it into the incisions. Season with salt and pepper. Put the rosemary sprigs in the roasting tin and put the lamb on top. Pour in the wine and add the remaining juniper berries.

■ Cover the roasting tin with foil and bring to the boil, then cook in a preheated oven, 160°C (325°F), Gas Mark 3, for 1 hour, turning the lamb every 20 minutes. Raise the temperature to 200°C (400°F), Gas Mark 6, uncover and roast for a further 30 minutes until the lamb is very tender.

ADD CITRUS

For leg of lamb with lemon & rosemary, omit the juniper berries and pound the grated zest of 2 lemons, with the garlic, anchovies and rosemary. Replace the vinegar with the juice of 1 lemon. Spoon the sauce over the lamb, and cook as for the main recipe.

Preparation time 10 minutes
Cooking time 10 minutes

INGREDIENTS

1	4 veal escalopes, about 150 g (5 oz) each
2	4 slices of Parma ham
3	4 sage leaves
4	150 ml (¼ pint) dry white wine
5	400 g (13 oz) green beans

STORECUPBOARD

plain flour, for dusting; 2 tablespoons olive oil; salt and black pepper

Veal Escalopes with Parma Ham

■ Lay the escalopes between 2 sheets of clingfilm and beat with a rolling pin until wafer thin.

■ Season with salt and pepper, then lay a slice of Parma ham on each escalope, followed by a sage leaf. Secure the sage and ham in position with a cocktail stick, then lightly dust both sides of the veal with flour. Season again with salt and pepper.

■ Melt the oil in a large frying pan over a high heat. Add the escalopes and cook for 2–3 minutes on each side until golden brown. Add the wine to the pan and bubble until thickened and reduced by about half. Serve immediately, accompanied by steamed green beans.

TRY A CHICKEN VERSION

For chicken breast with rosemary & pancetta, replace the veal with 4 boneless chicken breasts, about 150 g (5 oz) each, skinned. Top each flattened breast with a scattering of rosemary needles, then wrap each in a slice of pancetta, in place of the Parma ham, omitting the sage. Dust with flour, season with salt and pepper and cook as for the main recipe.

SERVES 6

Preparation time 10 minutes, plus resting
Cooking time 1¾ hours

INGREDIENTS

1 25 g (1 oz) butter

2 1 loin of pork with 6 chops, about 2.25 kg (4½ lb) in total, chined and skin removed (ask your butcher to do this for you)

3 1 litre (1¾ pints) milk

4 8 sage leaves

STORECUPBOARD

3 tablespoons olive oil; 4 garlic cloves, peeled but kept whole; pared rind of 2 lemons; salt and black pepper

Pork Braised in Milk

■ Melt the butter with the oil in a large, heavy-based flameproof casserole or a roasting tin large enough to hold the pork. Season the pork with salt and pepper and add to the pan, fat-side down. Cook over a medium-high heat for 10 minutes until golden brown.

■ Pour away most of the fat and turn the pork over, skin-side up. Pour in the milk and add the garlic, lemon rind and sage. Bring to the boil, then cover with a lid or foil, leaving a little gap for the steam to escape. Cook on the hob over a very low heat or in a preheated oven, 150°C (300°F), Gas Mark 2, for 1½ hours, basting regularly with the sauce. The pork is ready when the meat feels very tender when pierced with a fork.

■ Remove the meat and leave to rest for 10 minutes.

■ The sauce, which should be biscuity in colour, will be unattractively lumpy, so vigorously whisk to break up the lumps or process in a food processor or blender until smooth. Reheat if necessary and season with salt and pepper. Separate the loin into 6 chops and serve with the sauce spooned over.

SERVES 4

Preparation time 10 minutes, plus resting
Cooking time about 1 hour

INGREDIENTS

1 4 large thyme sprigs

2 3 large rosemary sprigs

3 1 organic or free-range chicken, about
1.75 kg (3½ lb)

STORECUPBOARD

8 garlic cloves, unpeeled; 1 tablespoon olive oil; salt
and black pepper

Roast Chicken with Herbs & Garlic

■ Put the garlic cloves and half the herb sprigs in the body cavity of the chicken. Pat the chicken dry with kitchen paper and rub the oil all over the outside of the bird. Strip the leaves off the remaining herb sprigs and rub over the bird, with a little salt and pepper.

■ Place the chicken, breast-side up, in a roasting tin. Roast in a preheated oven, 220°C (425°F), Gas Mark 7, for 10 minutes. Turn the chicken over, breast-side down, reduce the oven temperature to 180°C (350°F), Gas Mark 4, and cook for a further 20 minutes. Finally, turn the chicken back to its original position and roast for another 25 minutes until the skin is crisp and golden. Check that the chicken is cooked by piercing the thigh with a knife. The juices should run clear, with no sign of pink. If not, cook for a further 10 minutes.

■ Transfer to a warmed serving plate and leave to rest for 5 minutes before serving with the pan juices.

SERVES 4

Preparation time 10 minutes
Cooking time 15 minutes

INGREDIENTS

1   4 radicchio di treviso or 2 round radicchio

2   8 slices of speck

3   75 g (3 oz) Fontina cheese, thinly sliced

STORECUPBOARD

2 tablespoons olive oil; salt and black pepper

Grilled Radicchio, Fontina & Speck

■ Cut the radicchio di treviso in half lengthways. If using round radicchio, cut into quarters. Brush all sides of the radicchio with the oil, then season with salt and pepper. Arrange on a baking sheet and cook under a preheated medium grill, about 12 cm (5 in) from the heat source, for 10 minutes, until slightly softened. The leaves will darken in colour, but they should not char, so reduce the heat or increase the distance between the radicchio and the heat source if necessary.

■ Drape each piece of radicchio with a slice of speck, then top with the Fontina. Grill for a further 2 minutes until the cheese has melted and serve.

SERVES 4

Preparation time 10 minutes, plus resting
Cooking time 10–20 minutes

INGREDIENTS

1	about 750 g (1½ lb) lamb loin roast, trimmed of fat
2	a few small sprigs of rosemary plus 1 tablespoon chopped rosemary
3	350 g (11½ oz) fresh tagliatelle

STORECUPBOARD

4 garlic cloves, cut into slivers; 2 red onions, quartered; 50 ml (2 fl oz) olive oil; salt and black pepper

Lamb with Rosemary Oil

■ Make small incisions all over the lamb loin and insert the garlic slivers and rosemary sprigs.

■ Place the meat in a preheated hot griddle pan and cook, turning occasionally, until seared all over for about 10 minutes for rare or about 20 minutes for well done.

■ Add the onions half-way through the cooking and char on the outside. Let the lamb rest for 5 minutes, then carve into slices.

■ Meanwhile, put the oil and chopped rosemary in a mortar and crush with a pestle to release the flavours. Season with salt and pepper.

■ Spoon the rosemary oil over the lamb and serve at once with the fried onions and fresh tagliatelle.

SERVES 4

Preparation time 20 minutes
Cooking time 28–30 minutes

INGREDIENTS

1 1 tablespoon chopped thyme plus thyme, leaves or flowers, to garnish

2 4 pork chops, about 200 g (7 oz) each

3 1 kg (2 lb) floury potatoes, peeled and quartered

4 200 ml (7 fl oz) double cream

5 50 g (2 oz) butter

STORECUPBOARD

finely grated rind of 1 lemon; 2 tablespoons olive oil; 2 garlic cloves, crushed; salt and black pepper

Pork Chops with Lemon & Thyme

■ Mix together the lemon rind, thyme, oil, garlic and plenty of pepper and rub the mixture over the pork chops. Set aside.

■ Meanwhile, cook the potatoes in lightly salted boiling water for about 20 minutes or until soft. Drain, return to the pan and mash. Add the cream, butter and seasoning and use a electric hand-held whisk to beat until smooth.

■ Heat a dry frying pan over a medium-high heat and cook the pork chops for 4–5 minutes on each side, depending on their thickness, until cooked and golden.

■ Remove the pork from the heat and leave to rest for 1–2 minutes before serving garnished with a few thyme leaves or flowers and accompanied by the fluffy mash.

SERVES 4

Preparation time 10 minutes, plus resting
Cooking time 55 minutes

INGREDIENTS

1	50 g (2 oz) butter
2	2 tablespoons oregano, chopped
3	2 poussins, about 500 g (1 lb) each
4	150 g (5 oz) peppery mixed salad leaves

STORECUPBOARD

finely grated rind of 1 lemon; 1 large garlic clove,
crushed; salt and black pepper

Roast Poussins with Oregano

■ Mash together the butter, lemon rind,
oregano, garlic and seasoning. Lift the skin
from the poussins and slide the flavoured
butter between the flesh and skin, or, if you
prefer, smear the butter over the skin.

■ Put the poussins side by side in a
roasting tin and cook in a preheated
oven, 220°C (425°F), Gas Mark 7, for about
55 minutes, basting occasionally, until
golden and crispy and the juices run clear.
Remove from the oven and leave to rest for
5 minutes.

■ Transfer the poussins to a chopping
board and use a long, sharp knife to cut
each one carefully in half lengthways. Serve
immediately with the salad leaves.

Preparation time 10 minutes, plus standing
Cooking time 35 minutes

INGREDIENTS

1   50 g (2 oz) butter

2   150 g (5 oz) pancetta, cubed

3   200 g (7 oz) pack vacuum-packed cooked chestnuts

4   150 g (5 oz) arborio, carnaroli or vialone nano rice

5   150 ml (¼ pint) milk

STORECUPBOARD

1 onion, finely chopped; 500 ml (17 fl oz) chicken stock; salt and black pepper

Chestnut, Rice & Pancetta Soup

■ Melt half the butter in a saucepan over a medium heat. Add the pancetta and onion and cook for 10 minutes. Cut the chestnuts in half and add to the pan with the rice and stock. Bring to the boil, then reduce the heat and simmer, stirring occasionally, for 20 minutes, or until most of the liquid has been absorbed and the rice is tender.

■ Heat the milk in a small saucepan until tepid, then stir into the rice with the remaining butter and season the dish with salt and pepper. Cover and leave to stand for 5 minutes before serving.

SERVES 5-6

Preparation time 20 minutes
Cooking time 40 minutes

INGREDIENTS

1 1 kg (2 lb) veal, chopped into cubes

2 2 baby fennel bulbs, roughly chopped

3 300 ml (½ pint) white wine

4 4 bay leaves

5 1 tablespoon chopped thyme

STORECUPBOARD

2 tablespoons olive oil; 2 onions, sliced; 4 garlic cloves, sliced; 300 ml (½ pint) chicken stock; rind of ½ lemon, cut into julienne strips (matchsticks); salt and black pepper

Veal with Wine & Lemon

■ Heat the oil in a frying pan over a high heat, then fry off the meat in batches, draining to a plate with a slotted spoon.

■ Add the onions and garlic to the pan and cook over a medium heat until golden. Add the fennel and fry for a further 3-4 minutes or until softened.

■ Return the veal to the pan and add the wine, stock, lemon rind, bay leaves and thyme. Bring to the boil.

■ Reduce the heat and simmer, covered, for a further 20-25 minutes. Season to taste and serve.

SERVES 4

Preparation time 10 minutes
Cooking time 45 minutes

INGREDIENTS

1   2 tablespoons chopped thyme

2   4 chicken quarters, about 375 g
(12 oz) each

3   4 streaky bacon rashers, rind removed

4   150 ml (¼ pint) dry white wine

STORECUPBOARD

2 tablespoons extra virgin olive oil; 2 garlic
cloves, crushed; grated rind and juice of 1 lemon;
1 tablespoon plain flour; 300 ml (½ pint) chicken
stock; salt and black pepper

Herb & Bacon Chicken Roast

■ Combine the oil, thyme, garlic, lemon
rind and salt and pepper to taste in a bowl.
Score the chicken quarters several times
with a sharp knife and rub all over with the
oil and herb mixture. Wrap each chicken
quarter with bacon using cocktail sticks to
secure in place.

■ Transfer to a roasting tin and roast in
a preheated oven, 200°C (400°F), Gas
Mark 6, for 35–40 minutes until crisp and
golden. Remove from the oven, transfer the
chicken pieces to a warm platter and wrap
with foil.

■ Pour off all but 2 tablespoons fat
from the roasting tin and place the tin
over a medium heat. Add the flour and
cook, stirring constantly, for 30 seconds.
Gradually whisk in the wine and then
the stock and simmer for 5 minutes until
thickened. Serve with the chicken.

ROAST POTATOES

For perfect roast potatoes to serve
with the chicken, cook 750 g (1½ lb)
peeled potatoes in a large saucepan
of lightly salted boiling water for
10 minutes. Drain well, return to
the pan and shake firmly to fluff up
the edges. Put 4 tablespoons olive
oil in a roasting tin and heat in a
preheated oven, 200°C (400°F),
Gas Mark 6, for 5 minutes. Carefully
tip in the potatoes (the oil will spit)
and roast in the oven for 45–50
minutes, stirring halfway through,
until crisp and golden.

MAKES 2

Preparation time 5 minutes
Cooking time 8–10 minutes

INGREDIENTS

1	2 large flour tortillas or flatbreads
2	4 tablespoons ready-made tomato pasta sauce
3	100 g (3½ oz) spicy salami slices
4	150 g (5 oz) mozzarella cheese, thinly sliced
5	1 tablespoon oregano leaves, plus extra to garnish

STORECUPBOARD

salt and black pepper

Tortilla Pizza with Salami

■ Lay the tortillas or flatbreads on 2 large baking sheets. Top each with half the pasta sauce, spreading it up to the edge. Arrange half the salami and mozzarella slices and oregano leaves over the top.

■ Bake in a preheated oven, 200°C (400°F), Gas Mark 6, for 8–10 minutes or until the cheese has melted and is golden. Serve garnished with extra oregano leaves.

SERVES 4

Preparation time 5 minutes
Cooking time 5 minutes

INGREDIENTS

1   3 sirloin steaks, about 300 g (10 oz) each

2   150 g (5 oz) radicchio, sliced into 2.5 cm (1 in) strips

STORECUPBOARD

½ tablespoon olive oil; 2 garlic cloves, finely chopped; salt

Beef Strips with Radicchio

■ Trim the fat from the steaks and slice the meat into very thin strips.

■ Heat the oil in a heavy-based frying pan over a high heat, add the garlic and steak strips, season with salt and stir-fry for 2 minutes or until the steak strips are golden brown.

■ Add the radicchio and stir-fry until the leaves are just beginning to wilt. Serve immediately.

SERVES 4

Preparation time 10 minutes
Cooking time 10 minutes

INGREDIENTS

1   4 mini pizza bases

2   250 g (8 oz) mozzarella cheese, shredded

3   8 cherry tomatoes, quartered

4   150 g (5 oz) prosciutto, sliced

5   50 g (2 oz) rocket leaves, washed

STORECUPBOARD

2 garlic cloves, halved; balsamic vinegar, to taste; salt and black pepper

Quick Prosciutto & Rocket Pizza

■ Rub the top surfaces of the pizza bases with the cut faces of the garlic cloves and discard the cloves.

■ Put the pizza bases on a baking sheet, top with mozzarella and tomatoes and bake in a preheated oven, 200°C (400°F), Gas Mark 6, for 10 minutes until the bread is golden.

■ Top the pizzas with prosciutto and rocket leaves, season to taste with salt, pepper and balsamic vinegar and serve immediately.

SERVES 4-6

Preparation time 15 minutes, plus resting
Cooking time 1 hour 50 minutes

INGREDIENTS

1	10 sage leaves
2	2 large rosemary sprigs
3	1 tablespoon fennel seeds
4	1 boned pork belly joint, about 1.25 kg (2½ lb)

STORECUPBOARD

3 garlic cloves, crushed; 4 tablespoons olive oil; salt and black pepper

Roast Herbed Pork Belly

■ Roughly chop the sage and rosemary and combine with the garlic, fennel seeds and half the oil in a small bowl.

■ Place the pork on a chopping board, skin-side up, and score the rind at 2.5 cm (1 in) intervals (the easiest way of doing this is with a Stanley knife). Turn the meat over, skin-side down, and season with salt and pepper. Rub the herb mixture all over the flesh. Roll the pork up and tie it tightly with string. Rub the skin all over with the remaining oil, then a generous amount of salt.

■ Roast in a preheated oven, 220°C (425°F), Gas Mark 7, for 20 minutes, then reduce the temperature to 160°C (325°F), Gas Mark 3, and roast for a further 1½ hours. Leave the meat to rest for 10 minutes before carving and serving.

A DIFFERENT STUFFING

For sausage & apricot stuffed pork, instead of the herb mixture, roughly chop 4 sage leaves and 6 ready-to-eat dried apricots, then stir into 150 g (5 oz) pork sausagemeat. Follow the main recipe from the second step onwards, spreading the sausagement mixture over the seasoned pork.

VEGETABLES

MAKES 1 LOAF (ABOUT 8 THICK SLICES)

Preparation time 25 minutes, plus 30 minutes proving
Cooking time 30 minutes

INGREDIENTS

1   1 teaspoon fast-action dried yeast

2   250 g (8 oz) chestnut mushrooms, thinly sliced

3   300 g (10 oz) mozzarella cheese, sliced

4   25 g (1 oz) basil leaves

5   2 teaspoons green peppercorns in brine, rinsed and drained

STORECUPBOARD

225 ml (7½ fl oz) water; 6 tablespoons extra-virgin olive oil; 1 teaspoon salt; 400 g (13 oz) strong white bread flour; sea salt, for sprinkling

Mushroom & Mozzarella Stromboli

■ If using a bread machine, lift out the pan and fit the blade. Put the yeast, measurement water, 3 tablespoons extra-virgin olive oil, salt and flour in the pan, following the order specified in the manual. Fit the pan into the machine and close the lid. Set to the dough program.

■ If making the dough by hand, put the flour, 1 teaspoon salt and the yeast into a bowl. Add the measurement water and 3 tablespoons of the olive oil and mix with a wooden spoon until a rough dough forms. Use your hands to bring it together into a ball. Place it on a lightly floured work surface and knead for about 10 minutes until you have a smooth, elastic dough.

■ Fry the mushrooms in 2 tablespoons of the remaining oil until golden. Leave to cool.

■ At the end of the program or kneading process turn the dough out on to a floured surface and roll it out to a 33 cm (13 in) square. Arrange the mozzarella slices, basil leaves and mushrooms over the dough. Lightly crush the peppercorns and scatter over the filling with a little salt.

■ Loosely roll up the dough and transfer to a large, greased baking sheet with the join underneath. Pinch the ends together to seal. Cover loosely with oiled clingfilm and leave in a warm place for 30 minutes.

■ Flour a large skewer or meat fork and pierce the dough all over, making sure you go right through to the baking sheet. Drizzle with the remaining tablespoon oil and sprinkle with sea salt. Bake in a preheated oven, 220°C (425°F), Gas Mark 7, for about 25 minutes until risen and golden. Serve warm or cold.

SERVES 4

Preparation time 15 minutes, plus standing
Cooking time 35 minutes

INGREDIENTS

1	**4 large or 8 small tomatoes, about 625 g (1¼ lb) in total**
2	**75 g (3 oz) arborio, carnaroli or vialone nano rice**
3	**6 basil leaves, torn**

STORECUPBOARD

2 garlic cloves, crushed; 2 tablespoons extra virgin olive oil, plus extra for oiling and drizzling; salt and black pepper

Tomatoes Stuffed with Rice

■ Cut a slice off the stalk end of each tomato and set aside to use as lids. Scoop the pulp out of the tomatoes and chop. Transfer to a large bowl, taking care not to lose any of the tomato juices, and add the garlic, rice and basil. Season with salt and pepper and stir in 1 tablespoon of the oil. Cover and leave to stand at room temperature for 1 hour, for the rice to soak up all the juices.

■ Stuff the tomatoes with the rice mixture, then transfer to an oiled baking dish. Top with their reserved lids and drizzle with the remaining oil. Bake in a preheated oven, 180°C (350°F), Gas Mark 4, for 35 minutes until the tomatoes are soft and the rice is cooked through. Serve warm or at room temperature.

SERVES 3–4

Preparation time 5 minutes
Cooking time 10 minutes

INGREDIENTS

1 500 g (1 lb) potato gnocchi

2 150 g (5 oz) Gorgonzola cheese, cut into small pieces

3 3 tablespoons double cream

4 plenty of freshly grated nutmeg

5 250 g (8 oz) baby leaf spinach

STORECUPBOARD

300 ml (½ pint) vegetable stock; black pepper

Spinach & Gorgonzola Gnocchi

■ Bring the stock to the boil in a large saucepan. Tip in the gnocchi and return to the boil. Cook for 2–3 minutes or until plumped up and tender.

■ Stir in the cheese, cream and nutmeg and heat until the cheese melts to make a creamy sauce.

■ Add the spinach to the pan and cook gently for 1–2 minutes, turning the spinach with the gnocchi and sauce until wilted. Pile on to serving plates and season with plenty of pepper.

SERVES 4

Preparation time 10 minutes, plus cooling
Cooking time 15 minutes

INGREDIENTS

1   2 red peppers

2   8 spring onions, finely sliced

3   500 g (1 lb) fresh cheese-stuffed tortellini or any other fresh stuffed tortellini of your choice

4   25 g (1 oz) Parmesan cheese, finely grated

STORECUPBOARD

2 garlic cloves, chopped; 175 ml (6 fl oz) olive oil; salt and black pepper

Red Pepper & Cheese Tortellini

■ Cut the peppers into large pieces, removing the cores and seeds. Lay skin-side up under a preheated grill and cook until the skin blackens and blisters. Transfer to a plastic bag, tie the top to enclose and leave to cool, then peel away the skin.

■ Place the peppers and garlic in a food processor and blend until fairly smooth. Stir in the spring onions and set aside.

■ Cook the tortellini in a large saucepan of boiling water according to the packet instructions until al dente. Drain and return to the pan.

■ Toss the pepper mixture into the pasta to combine and add the oil and Parmesan. Season to taste with salt and pepper and serve immediately.

SERVES 4

Preparation time 10 minutes
Cooking time about 25 minutes

INGREDIENTS

1 2 aubergines, sliced in half lengthways

2 250 g (8 oz) can chopped tomatoes

3 1 tablespoon tomato purée

4 300 g (10 oz) mozzarella cheese, cut into thin slices

5 basil, to garnish

STORECUPBOARD

3 tablespoons olive oil; 1 onion, chopped; 1 garlic clove, crushed; salt and black pepper

Baked Aubergines & Mozzarella

■ Brush the aubergines with 2 tablespoons of the oil and arrange, cut-side up, on a baking sheet. Roast in a preheated oven, 200°C (400°F), Gas Mark 6, for 20 minutes.

■ Meanwhile, heat the remaining oil in a frying pan, add the onion and garlic and cook until the onion is soft and starting to brown. Add the tomatoes and tomato purée and simmer for 5 minutes or until the sauce has thickened.

■ Remove the aubergines from the oven and cover each half with some sauce and the mozzarella slices. Season to taste with salt and pepper and return to the oven for 4–5 minutes to melt the cheese. Serve immediately scattered with basil leaves.

Preparation time 10 minutes
Cooking time 10 minutes

INGREDIENTS

1   400 g (13 oz) fresh tagliatelle

2   6 vine-ripened tomatoes, deseeded and chopped

3   25 g (1 oz) basil leaves

STORECUPBOARD

5 tablespoons olive oil; 5 garlic cloves, finely chopped; salt and black pepper

Pasta with Tomato & Basil Sauce

■ Cook the pasta in a large saucepan of salted boiling water according to the packet instructions.

■ Meanwhile, heat 3 tablespoons olive oil in a frying pan, add the garlic and cook over a low heat for 1 minute. When the garlic begins to change colour, remove the pan from the heat and add the remaining oil.

■ Drain the pasta and return to the pan. Add the garlic oil with the chopped tomatoes and basil leaves. Season to taste with salt and pepper and toss well to mix. Serve immediately.

SERVES 4

Preparation time 5 minutes
Cooking time 35 minutes

INGREDIENTS

1	50 g (2 oz) butter
2	300 g (10 oz) arborio, carnaroli or vialone nano rice
3	150 ml (¼ pint) dry white wine
4	½ teaspoon saffron threads
5	4 tablespoons freshly grated Parmesan cheese, plus extra to serve

STORECUPBOARD

1 onion, finely chopped; 1 litre (1¾ pints) beef or vegetable stock, simmering

Saffron Risotto

■ Melt half the butter in a heavy-based saucepan over a low heat. Add the onion and cook for 10 minutes until softened. Add the rice and cook, stirring, for 1 minute. Pour in the wine and cook, stirring, until absorbed.

■ Add 2 ladlefuls of the simmering stock and the saffron. Slowly simmer, stirring constantly, until the stock has been absorbed and the rice parts when a wooden spoon is run through it. Add another ladleful of stock and continue to cook, stirring and adding the stock in ladlefuls, for 18–20 minutes until the rice is creamy and almost tender to the bite.

■ Remove from the heat and stir in the Parmesan and remaining butter. Stir vigorously for 15 seconds. Cover with a tight-fitting lid and leave to stand for 1 minute. Serve immediately with extra Parmesan on the side.

Preparation time 15 minutes
Cooking time 35 minutes

INGREDIENTS

1   200 g (7 oz) cherry tomatoes

2   large pinch of crushed dried chillies

3   ready-made pizza dough

4   150 g (5 oz) buffalo mozzarella cheese, drained and torn into large pieces

5   50 g (2 oz) wild rocket leaves

STORECUPBOARD

2 garlic cloves, crushed; 2 tablespoons olive oil, plus extra for glazing; plain flour, for dusting; salt

Cherry Tomato & Rocket Pizza

■ Put the tomatoes in a large bowl and crush them between your fingers. Add the garlic and crushed chillies, then stir in half the oil. Season with salt, cover and leave to infuse.

■ Roll out the pizza dough into 4 rounds, about 1 cm (½ inch) thick. Transfer the first pizza base to a floured baking sheet and spoon a quarter of the tomato mixture over, then brush the border with oil to glaze. Place in a preheated oven, 240°C (475°F), Gas Mark 9. Bake for 8 minutes until crisp. Scatter with a quarter each of the mozzarella and rocket and serve immediately. As the first pizza cooks, prepare the next for the oven.

Preparation time 10 minutes
Cooking time 15 minutes

INGREDIENTS

1 500 g (1 lb) broccoli, roughly chopped

2 400 g (13 oz) dried orecchiette

3 2 anchovy fillets in olive oil, drained and roughly chopped

4 large pinch of crushed dried chillies

5 4 tablespoons freshly grated Parmesan cheese, plus extra to serve

STORECUPBOARD

5 tablespoons extra virgin olive oil; 2 garlic cloves, sliced

Orecchiette with Broccoli

■ Bring a large saucepan of salted water to the boil and tip in the broccoli and pasta. Cook for about 14 minutes, or according to the pasta packet instructions, until the pasta is al dente and the broccoli is cooked and starting to fall apart.

■ Meanwhile, pour the oil into a large frying pan and add the anchovies, crushed chillies and garlic and heat over a very low heat for 5–6 minutes until the anchovies have melted into the oil.

■ Drain the pasta, reserving a ladleful of the cooking water, and toss the pasta and broccoli into the pan with the anchovy oil. Toss over a high heat for 30 seconds, then pour in the reserved cooking water and continue stirring over the heat for a further 30 seconds. Work the Parmesan into the pasta, then serve with an extra scattering of Parmesan.

SERVES 4

Preparation time 5 minutes
Cooking time 15 minutes

INGREDIENTS

1	225 g (7½ oz) instant polenta
2	50 g (2 oz) butter, plus extra for greasing
3	200 g (7 oz) Gorgonzola cheese, broken into pieces
4	5 tablespoons freshly grated Parmesan cheese
5	10 cherry tomatoes

STORECUPBOARD

750 ml (1¼ pints) water; salt and black pepper

Baked Polenta with Gorgonzola

■ Bring the measurement water to the boil in a large, heavy-based saucepan. Set aside 2 tablespoons of the polenta to use for the topping and put the remaining polenta in a jug. Pour into the water in a slow but steady stream, stirring vigorously with a wooden spoon to prevent any lumps forming. Reduce the heat to a slow simmer and cook, stirring frequently, for about 5 minutes, or until the polenta is thick and comes away from the side of the pan. Stir in the butter and season with salt and pepper.

■ Grease a 25 × 18 cm (10 × 7 in) baking dish and pour half the polenta into it. Top with the Gorgonzola and half the Parmesan. Cover with the remaining cooked polenta, then top with the tomatoes. Stir the remaining Parmesan into the reserved uncooked polenta for the topping and scatter over the dish.

■ Cook under a preheated medium grill for 4–5 minutes until the tomatoes are slightly softened and beginning to char. Serve steaming hot.

SERVES 4

Preparation time 30 minutes
Cooking time 1 hour

INGREDIENTS

1	6 baby globe artichokes
2	2 shallots, thinly sliced
3	500 g (1 lb) potatoes, peeled and cut into 3.5 cm (1½ in) chunks
4	100 g (3½ oz) shelled fresh or frozen peas
5	handful of flat leaf parsley, roughly chopped

STORECUPBOARD

juice of 1 lemon; 4 tablespoons olive oil; 1 garlic clove, finely chopped; salt and black pepper

Braised Artichokes & Potatoes

■ Trim the stalks of the artichokes, leaving about 3 cm (1¼ in). Pull off and discard the tough outer leaves, exposing the paler tender leaves, then cut off their tips. Using a potato peeler, peel the stalk and dark green base until you see the lighter, yellowy flesh. Halve the artichokes and scoop out the hairy choke with a teaspoon and discard. Put in a bowl of cold water with the lemon juice to prevent discolouring.

■ Heat the oil in a large, heavy-based saucepan with a tight-fitting lid just large enough to hold the artichokes and potatoes in a single layer. Add the shallots and cook over a medium heat for 8–10 minutes until softened and translucent. Add the garlic and cook, stirring, for 1 minute. Toss in the drained artichokes, potatoes and salt and pepper.

■ Pour in enough water to come a quarter of the way up the vegetables. Bring to the boil, then reduce to a slow simmer. Cover with greaseproof paper and the lid. Cook for 45 minutes. Stir in the peas and parsley and cook for a further 5 minutes, or until the artichokes and potatoes are tender.

SERVES 1

Preparation time 10 minutes
Cooking time 4–5 minutes

INGREDIENTS

1   40 g (1½ oz) ricotta cheese

2   1 tomato, finely chopped

3   ¼ green chilli, deseeded and finely chopped

4   1 tablespoon chopped fresh coriander

5   2 small soft flour tortillas

STORECUPBOARD

½ red onion, thinly sliced; olive oil, for brushing

Ricotta & Red Onion Tortillas

■ Mix together the ricotta, onion, tomato, chilli and coriander in a bowl.

■ Heat a ridged griddle pan until hot. Brush the tortillas with a little oil, add to the pan and cook very briefly on each side.

■ Spread half the ricotta mixture over one half of each tortilla and fold over the other half to cover. Serve immediately with a green salad, if liked.

SERVES 4

Preparation time 5 minutes
Cooking time 5–10 minutes

INGREDIENTS

1   300 g (10 oz) fresh or dried fusilli

2   125 g (4 oz) pine nuts

3   75 g (3 oz) butter

4   handful of basil leaves

5   75 g (3 oz) Parmesan cheese, grated

STORECUPBOARD

2 tablespoons olive oil; salt and black pepper

Fusilli with Parmesan & Pine Nuts

■ Cook the pasta in a large saucepan of salted boiling water or according to the packet instructions until al dente.

■ Meanwhile, toast the pine nuts on a grill pan under a preheated medium grill or in a dry frying pan over a medium heat. Watch them constantly and move them around to brown evenly. Melt the butter with the oil in a small saucepan.

■ Drain the pasta and return to the pan. Stir in half the basil leaves so they start to wilt, add the melted butter and oil, season with salt and pepper and toss well.

■ Transfer to warmed serving plates, sprinkle with the pine nuts, Parmesan and the remaining basil leaves and serve immediately.

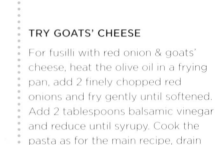

TRY GOATS' CHEESE

For fusilli with red onion & goats' cheese, heat the olive oil in a frying pan, add 2 finely chopped red onions and fry gently until softened. Add 2 tablespoons balsamic vinegar and reduce until syrupy. Cook the pasta as for the main recipe, drain and stir in the red onion mixture. Spoon into serving bowls, crumble over 200 g (7 oz) goats' cheese and sprinkle with the basil leaves.

SERVES 4

Preparation time 5 minutes
Cooking time 20 minutes

INGREDIENTS

1	2 leeks, cut into 1 cm (½ in) pieces
2	1 orange pepper, deseeded and cut into 1 cm (½ in) chunks
3	1 red pepper, deseeded and cut into 1 cm (½ in) chunks
4	3 tablespoons balsamic vinegar
5	handful of flat leaf parsley, chopped

STORECUPBOARD

2 tablespoons olive oil; salt and black pepper

Balsamic Braised Leeks & Peppers

■ Heat the oil in a saucepan, add the leeks and orange and red peppers and stir well. Cover the pan and cook very gently for 10 minutes. Add the balsamic vinegar and cook for a further 10 minutes without a lid. The vegetables should be brown from the vinegar and all the liquid should have evaporated.

■ Season well, then stir in the chopped parsley just before serving.

SERVES 4

Preparation time 10 minutes
Cooking time 25 minutes

INGREDIENTS

1   150 g (5 oz) baby spinach

2   125 g (4 oz) shelled fresh or frozen peas

3   6 eggs

STORECUPBOARD

1 tablespoon olive oil; 1 onion, thinly sliced; salt and black pepper

Spinach & Pea Frittata

■ Heat the oil in a heavy-based, ovenproof, nonstick 23 cm (9 in) frying pan over a low heat. Add the onion and cook for 6–8 minutes until softened, then stir in the spinach and peas and cook for a further 2 minutes, or until any moisture released by the spinach has evaporated.

■ Beat the eggs in a bowl and season lightly with salt and pepper. Stir in the cooked vegetables, then pour the mixture into the pan and quickly arrange the vegetables so that they are evenly dispersed. Cook over a low heat for 8–10 minutes, or until all but the top of the frittata is set.

■ Transfer the pan to a preheated, very hot grill and cook about 10 cm (4 in) from the heat source until the top is set but not yet coloured.

■ Give the pan a gentle shake to loosen the frittata, then transfer the frittata to a plate to cool. Serve the frittata slightly warm or at room temperature.

SWEETS

SERVES 4

Preparation time 10 minutes, plus whisking or churning and freezing
Cooking time 5 minutes

INGREDIENTS

1 150 g (5 oz) blanched hazelnuts

2 350 g (11½ oz) hazelnut and chocolate spread

3 400 g (13 oz) can evaporated milk

Hazelnut Chocolate Ice Cream

■ Roughly crush the hazelnuts, then toast in a frying pan over a low heat until lightly golden. Leave to cool.

■ Spoon the spread into a bowl and stir in a quarter of the evaporated milk until you have a smooth mixture. Stir in the remaining evaporated milk, then fold in 100 g (3½ oz) toasted hazelnuts.

■ Churn in an ice-cream machine according to the manufacturer's instructions. Transfer to a plastic freezerproof container and freeze.

■ Alternatively, freeze the mixture in a shallow container or tray for 2 hours until half-frozen, then tip into a bowl and whisk thoroughly to break up any ice crystals that may have formed. Return the mixture to the container and the freezer. Repeat the process at hourly intervals until the mixture

is smooth and almost set. Finally, transfer the ice cream to a plastic freezerproof container and freeze until firm.

■ Remove the ice cream from the freezer 10 minutes before serving to soften slightly; it is best eaten within 48 hours. Scatter with the remaining hazelnuts and serve.

SERVES 4

Preparation time 10 minutes
Cooking time 10 minutes

INGREDIENTS

1. 500 g (1 lb) strawberries, halved or quartered, depending on size

2. 3 egg yolks

3. 6 tablespoons dry or sweet sherry

STORECUPBOARD

50 g (2 oz) caster sugar; 4 teaspoons icing sugar

Grilled Strawberry Zabaglione

■ Divide the strawberries among 4 shallow 300 ml (½ pint) ovenproof dishes, or use a large 1.2 litre (2 pint) dish if preferred.

■ Put the egg yolks, sugar and 4 tablespoons of the sherry in a large bowl and set over a pan of simmering water. Cook the mixture, whisking continuously using a hand-held electric whisk (or rotary hand or balloon whisk), for 5 minutes until the mixture is very thick and frothy and almost half-fills the bowl.

■ Add the remaining sherry and cook for a few more minutes until thick once more. Pour the mixture over the strawberries and sift the icing sugar over the top.

■ Cook under a preheated hot grill for 3–4 minutes until golden or caramelize the sugar with a cook's blowtorch. Serve immediately.

MAKES 18-20

Preparation time 15 minutes, plus cooling
Cooking time 15-20 minutes

INGREDIENTS

1 125 g (4 oz) unsalted butter, diced and softened

2 2 egg yolks

3 100 g (3½ oz) coarse cornmeal

4 saffron, to sprinkle (optional)

STORECUPBOARD

125 g (4 oz) caster sugar; 2 teaspoons grated lemon rind; 150 g (5 oz) plain flour; icing sugar, for dusting

Lemon Cookies

■ Line a baking sheet with nonstick baking paper. In a bowl, beat the butter and caster sugar together until light and fluffy. Mix in the egg yolks, lemon rind, flour and cornmeal until a soft dough forms.

■ Roll out the dough on a lightly floured surface to 1 cm (½ in) thick. Using a 6 cm (2½ in) round cutter, cut out rounds from the dough, re-rolling the trimmings. Transfer to the prepared baking sheet, then sprinkle with saffron, if liked, and bake in a preheated oven, 160°C (325°F), Gas Mark 3, for 15-20 minutes or until lightly golden. Transfer to a wire rack to cool, then dust with icing sugar.

TURN THEM INTO CHEESECAKES

For no-cook lemon cheesecakes, roughly crush 10 of the biscuits from the main recipe and place them in the base of 4 dessert bowls or glasses. Whisk together 300 g (10 oz) cream cheese with the finely grated zest and juice of 1 lemon, 150 g (5 oz) caster sugar and 150 ml (¼ pint) double cream. Spoon this mixture into the prepared glasses and chill for 1–2 hours before serving.

SERVES 4

Preparation time 20 minutes, plus chilling
Cooking time 55–65 minutes

INGREDIENTS

1 2 tablespoons cocoa powder

2 2 eggs plus 2 egg yolks

3 65 g (2½ oz) amaretti biscuits, finely crushed, plus extra to decorate

4 450 ml (¾ pint) milk

5 150 ml (¼ pint) strong black coffee

STORECUPBOARD

175 g (6 oz) granulated sugar; 125 ml (4 fl oz) cold water; 4 tablespoons boiling water

Amaretti & Chocolate Custard

■ In a saucepan, dissolve 125 g (4 oz) sugar in the cold water, occasionally stirring. When dissolved, increase the heat and boil for 5 minutes without stirring until golden brown, keeping a watchful eye towards the end of the cooking time to make sure the mixture does not burn.

■ Mix the cocoa in a small bowl with 2 tablespoons of the boiling water. Mix the remaining sugar with the eggs, egg yolks and biscuits in a second larger bowl.

■ Take the syrup off the heat as soon as it caramelizes. Add the remaining boiling water and tilt to mix. Pour into a 900 ml (1½ pint) ovenproof dish. Tilt to coat the base and halfway up the sides. Stand in a roasting tin.

■ Pour the milk into the drained caramel pan and bring just to the boil. Stir the cocoa mix into the egg mixture, then gradually whisk in the hot milk, then the coffee. Slowly pour into the caramel-lined dish.

■ Fill the tin with hot water halfway up the sides of the dish, then cook in a preheated oven, 160°C (325°F), Gas Mark 3, for 50–60 minutes until the custard has just set but still wobbles slightly in the centre.

■ Take dish out of tin, leave to cool, then chill for 4–5 hours or overnight. To turn out, stand in just-boiled water for 10 seconds, then invert on a plate with a rim. Decorate with extra amaretti biscuits or chocolate curls, if liked.

SERVES 4-6

Preparation time 25 minutes, plus chilling, churning and freezing
Cooking time about 20 minutes

INGREDIENTS

1	pared rind of 2 blood oranges
2	300 ml (½ pint) blood orange juice
3	chilled Campari, to serve (optional)
4	orange rind, to decorate

STORECUPBOARD

250 g (8 oz) caster sugar; 250 ml (8 fl oz) water

Blood-orange Sorbet

■ Heat the sugar over a low heat in a small saucepan with the measurement water, stirring occasionally until completely dissolved.

■ Add the blood orange rind and increase the heat. Without stirring, boil the syrup for about 12 minutes and then set aside to cool completely.

■ When the syrup is cold, strain the sugar syrup over the orange juice, reserving the orange rind for decoration, and stir together. Refrigerate for about 2 hours until really cold.

■ Pour the chilled orange syrup into an ice cream machine and churn for about 10 minutes. When the sorbet is almost frozen, scrape it into a plastic container and put it in the freezer compartment for a further hour until completely frozen.

Alternatively, pour the chilled orange syrup into a shallow metal container and put it in the freezer for 2 hours. Remove and whisk with a hand-held electric whisk or balloon whisk, breaking up all the ice crystals. Return it to the freezer and repeat this process every hour or so until frozen.

■ Serve scoops of sorbet with a splash of chilled Campari, if liked, and decorate with thin strips of orange rind.

SERVES 6-8

Preparation time 20 minutes, plus chilling
Cooking time 20–25 minutes

INGREDIENTS

1   125 g (4 oz) unsalted butter, diced

2   1 egg and 1 egg yolk, lightly beaten

3   250 g (8 oz) low-sugar apricot jam

STORECUPBOARD

275 g (9 oz) plain flour, plus extra for dusting;
75 g (3 oz) caster sugar; icing sugar, for dusting

Apricot Jam Tart

■ Put the flour and caster sugar in a bowl, add the butter and rub in with your fingertips until the mixture resembles coarse breadcrumbs. Gradually mix in enough of the eggs to bring the pastry together. Knead very lightly into a dough. Cover with clingfilm and chill for 30–45 minutes.

■ Roll two-thirds of the pastry out on a lightly floured work surface. Use to line a shallow, 23 cm (9 in) fluted tart tin, then fill with the jam. Roll the remaining pastry out to a thickness of about 5 mm (¼ in), then cut strips about 1 cm (½ in) wide. Lightly brush the rim of the pastry case with water. Arrange the pastry strips in a lattice pattern over the tart. Chill for 20 minutes until firm.

■ Bake on a baking sheet in a preheated oven, 200°C (400°F), Gas Mark 6, for 20–25 minutes until the pastry is firm and golden. Leave to cool on a wire rack, then remove from the tin and serve with a generous dusting of icing sugar. The tart will keep in an airtight container for up to 2 days.

MAKE IT CHOCOLATEY

For chocolate & raspberry jam tart, reduce the quantity of flour in the pastry to 200 g (7 oz) and stir in 75 g (3 oz) cocoa powder with the sugar before rubbing in the butter. Use the pastry to line the tin as for the main recipe, then fill with 250 g (8 oz) low-sugar raspberry jam instead of the apricot. Finish the tart and bake as for the main recipe.

SERVES 8

Preparation time 20 minutes
Cooking time 35 minutes

INGREDIENTS

1. 125 g (4 oz) unsalted butter, softened, plus extra for greasing

2. 2 large eggs, beaten

3. 100 g (3½ oz) ground almonds

4. 3 ripe pears, peeled, halved and cored

5. 50 g (2 oz) flaked almonds

STORECUPBOARD

125 g (4 oz) caster sugar; 50 g (2 oz) plain flour, sifted; ½ teaspoon baking powder; icing sugar, for dusting

Pear & Almond Cake

■ Beat the butter and caster sugar together in a bowl until pale and fluffy. Add the eggs, a little at a time, beating well after each addition. If the mixture starts to curdle, add 1 tablespoon of the flour. Fold in the flour, ground almonds and baking powder using a large metal spoon and tip into a greased 20 cm (8 in) springform cake tin and use a palette knife to even out the mixture.

■ Arrange the pear halves over the top of the cake and bake in a preheated oven, 190°C (375°F), Gas Mark 5, for 25 minutes. Sprinkle the flaked almonds over the top and return to the oven for a further 10 minutes. The cake is ready when a skewer inserted into the centre of the cake comes out clean.

■ Leave the cake to cool in the tin, then carefully remove the ring and base. Dust with icing sugar before serving with Mascarpone, Marsala & Orange Cream (see opposite), if liked.

MAKE A FLAVOURED CREAM

For mascarpone, Marsala & orange cream to serve as an accompaniment, whisk the grated rind of 1 orange and 2 tablespoons of its juice in a bowl with 2 tablespoons sweet Marsala and 100 g (3½ oz) mascarpone cheese. Sweeten with icing sugar to taste.

SERVES 4

Preparation time 15 minutes, plus chilling and freezing
Cooking time 10 minutes

INGREDIENTS

1 65 g (2½ oz) unsweetened cocoa powder

2 25 g (1 oz) plain dark chocolate with 70% cocoa solids, finely chopped

3 2½ teaspoons vanilla extract

4 1 teaspoon instant espresso coffee powder

STORECUPBOARD

600 ml (1 pint) water; 150 g (5 oz) soft dark brown sugar; 200 g (7 oz) granulated sugar

Chocolate Sorbet

■ Put the measurement water, sugars and cocoa powder in a saucepan and mix together. Heat gently, stirring until the sugar has dissolved. Increase the heat to bring the mixture to a boil, then reduce to a simmer for 8 minutes.

■ Remove the pan from the heat and stir in the chocolate, vanilla extract and espresso powder until thoroughly dissolved. Pour into a bowl and cool over ice or leave to cool and chill.

■ If using an ice cream machine, pour the chilled chocolate mixture into it and churn for about 10 minutes. When the sorbet is almost frozen, scrape it into a plastic container and put it in the freezer for a further hour until completely frozen.

■ If not using a machine, pour the chilled chocolate mixture into a shallow metal container and put it in the freezer for 2 hours. Remove and whisk to break up all the ice crystals. Return it to the freezer and repeat this process hourly until frozen.

■ Transfer the sorbet to the refrigerator 20 minutes before serving to soften slightly. This will make it easier to scoop.

Preparation time 15 minutes, plus cooling
Cooking time 10 minutes

INGREDIENTS

1   40 g (1½ oz) amaretti biscuits

2   65 g (2½ oz) lightly salted butter, softened

3   1 egg

4   4 plums, stoned and chopped

5   8 unblanched almonds, chopped

STORECUPBOARD

40 g (1½ oz) light muscovado sugar; 65 g (2½ oz)
self-raising flour; ½ teaspoon baking powder;
50 g (2 oz) icing sugar, sifted; 2 teaspoons lemon juice

Amaretti Plum Cakes

■ Place 16 mini silicone muffin cases on a baking sheet.

■ Put the biscuits in a polythene bag and crush with a rolling pin until finely ground. Tip into a bowl and add the sugar, butter and egg, then sift in the flour and baking powder. Beat with a hand-held electric whisk until smooth and creamy. Divide among the cases.

■ Bake in a preheated oven, 180°C (350°F), Gas Mark 4, for 10 minutes, or until risen and just firm. Leave in the cases for 2 minutes, then transfer to a wire rack to cool completely.

■ Make the icing by beating the icing sugar with the lemon juice to make a smooth paste. Spread a little over the cakes and sprinkle over pieces of the chopped plums and almonds. Drizzle a little more icing on top.

TRY A GINGER VERSION

For apricot & ginger cakes, make the cakes as opposite, using crushed ginger nut biscuits instead of the amaretti and adding 1 finely chopped piece of preserved stem ginger in syrup. Use small apricots instead of the plums. After baking, drizzle the cakes with some of the stem ginger syrup instead of the icing.

SERVES 4

Preparation time 15 minutes

INGREDIENTS

1   750 g (1½ lb) ripe peaches, stoned

2   100 ml (3½ fl oz) sweet sparkling wine

3   15 ice cubes

STORECUPBOARD

juice of ½ lemon; 1 tablespoon icing sugar, plus extra to taste

Frozen Bellini

■ Put 500 g (1 lb) of the peaches in a blender and blend to a purée. Transfer to a large bowl. Slice the remaining fruit, put in a separate bowl and gently toss with the wine.

■ Whizz the lemon juice, icing sugar and ice cubes in the blender until the ice is well crushed – you may need to do this in stages to avoid overheating the blender.

■ Transfer the crushed ice mixture to the bowl with the puréed fruit and stir well to combine thoroughly. Taste, adding more icing sugar if necessary, and serve immediately, topped with the sliced fruit and wine.

TRY A NEW FLAVOUR

For strawberry & balsamic granita, replace the peaches with 625 g (1¼ lb) hulled strawberries. Purée 500 g (1 lb) of the strawberries, then quarter the remaining strawberries and stir into 2 tablespoons aged balsamic vinegar, instead of the sparkling wine. Complete as for the main recipe.

SERVES 4

Preparation time 10 minutes

INGREDIENTS

1	8 scoops of vanilla ice cream
2	4 freshly made espresso coffees
3	biscotti, to serve

Affogato Al Caffe

■ Pour a freshly made espresso coffee into each of 4 cappuccino cups or bowls.

■ Put 2 scoops of ice cream into each cup and serve immediately with biscotti.

MAKE IT MOCHA

For affogato al mocha, replace the vanilla ice cream with 8 scoops of rich, dark chocolate ice cream, add the coffee as for the main recipe and top with 50 g (2 oz) finely chopped plain dark chocolate.

SERVES 8–10

Preparation time 15 minutes, plus chilling
Cooking time 50–55 minutes

INGREDIENTS

1 350 g (11½ oz) ready-made sweet shortcrust pastry

2 4 eggs

3 350 g (11½ oz) ricotta cheese

4 400 ml (14 fl oz) double cream

5 fresh berries, to decorate

STORECUPBOARD

plain flour, for dusting; 100 g (3½ oz) caster sugar; rind and juice of 3 lemons

Lemon & Ricotta Tart

■ Roll the pastry out on a lightly floured work surface.

■ Use to line a 23 cm (9 in) fluted tart tin, then chill for 10 minutes. Line the pastry case with greaseproof paper and fill with baking beans.

■ Bake the pastry case in a preheated oven, 180°C (350°F), Gas Mark 4, for 10 minutes. Remove the baking beans and paper and bake for a further 5 minutes until golden.

■ Whisk the remaining ingredients together in a bowl and use to fill the pastry case. Reduce the oven temperature to 150°C (300°F), Gas Mark 2, and bake the tart for 35–40 minutes until just set. Serve with fresh berries, such as strawberries and blueberries.

SERVES 4

Preparation time 30 minutes, plus standing, cooling and chilling
Cooking time 15 minutes

INGREDIENTS

1	600 ml (1 pint) double cream
2	2 vanilla pods, split lengthways
3	4 tablespoons milk
4	1 tablespoon powdered gelatine
5	8 ripe apricots, halved, stoned and cut into thirds

STORECUPBOARD

200 g (7 oz) caster sugar; 75 ml (3 fl oz) granulated sugar; 150 ml (¼ pint) plus 2 tablespoons water

Caramel Panna Cotta & Apricots

■ Put the cream, 125 g (4 oz) of the caster sugar and a vanilla pod in a saucepan and heat until just below boiling point, stirring occasionally. Remove from the heat and leave to infuse for 20 minutes.

■ Meanwhile, heat the granulated sugar in 2 tablespoons water in a heavy-based saucepan until it has dissolved, then boil until the syrup turns to a golden caramel. Quickly pour into 4 × 150 ml (¼ pint) ramekins or small moulds. Set on a tray and leave to harden.

■ Pour the milk into a small saucepan and sprinkle on the gelatine. Warm over a low heat until the gelatine dissolves. Stir into the infused cream mixture. Bring to the boil, then immediately remove from the heat and strain through a sieve into a jug. Pour into the ramekins or moulds. Leave to cool, then for at least 5 hours, until set.

■ Put the apricots in a small saucepan with the 150 ml (¼ pint) water, remaining caster sugar and the second vanilla pod. Bring slowly to the boil, then cover and simmer gently for 5–8 minutes until just tender. Leave to cool, then remove the vanilla pod, cover and chill.

■ Carefully loosen the panna cottas and turn out on to individual serving plates. Serve with the apricots.

SERVES 4

Preparation time 10 minutes
Cooking time about 12 minutes

INGREDIENTS

1   4 egg yolks

2   150 ml (¼ pint) cream sherry

3   large pinch of ground cinnamon, plus extra to decorate

4   400 g (13 oz) can black cherries in syrup

5   amaretti biscuits, to serve

STORECUPBOARD

125 g (4 oz) caster sugar

Cherry & Cinnamon Zabaglione

■ Pour 5 cm (2 in) water into a medium saucepan and bring to the boil. Set a large heatproof bowl over the pan, making sure that the water does not touch the base of the bowl. Reduce the heat so that the water is simmering, then add the egg yolks, sugar, sherry and cinnamon to the bowl. Whisk for 5–8 minutes or until very thick and foamy and the custard leaves a trail when the whisk is lifted above the mixture.

■ Drain off some of the cherry syrup and then tip the cherries and just a little of the syrup into a small saucepan. Warm through, then spoon into 4 glasses. Pour the warm zabaglione over the top and dust with cinnamon. Serve with amaretti biscuits.

MAKES ABOUT 14

Preparation time 20 minutes
Cooking time 10 minutes

INGREDIENTS

| 1 | 150 g (5 oz) ground almonds |

| 2 | 1 egg white |

| 3 | ½ teaspoon vanilla extract |

STORECUPBOARD

1 tablespoon plain flour; 175 g (6 oz) caster sugar, plus extra for coating; ½ teaspoon baking powder

Almond Biscuits

■ Combine the almonds, flour, sugar and baking powder in a large bowl. Beat the egg white in a separate bowl until it holds its shape and has a consistency resembling shaving foam. Fold into the almond mixture. Add the vanilla extract and stir to combine thoroughly.

■ Dust a work surface with sugar. Roll 1 tablespoon of the biscuit dough in the palm of your hands to make a sausage shape about 6 cm (2½ in) long. Roll in the sugar, then place on a baking sheet lined with baking parchment. Repeat with the remaining dough to make about 14 biscuits. Make sure you leave plenty of space between each biscuit, as they spread during cooking.

■ Bake the biscuits in a preheated oven, 200°C (400°F), Gas Mark 6, for 10 minutes until lightly golden.

ADD SOME FRUIT

For candied fruit & sultana biscuits, prepare the biscuit dough as for the main recipe, but reduce the caster sugar to 150 g (5 oz) and stir in 2 tablespoons chopped candied peel, and 2 tablespoons sultanas with the vanilla extract. Shape into rolls, coat and bake as for the main recipe.

INDEX

PICTURE CREDITS

Special photography: Octopus Publishing Group/Jonathan Kennedy

All other photography:
Octopus Publishing Group 47; Stephen Conroy 5, 23, 29, 31, 33, 35, 43, 51, 53, 65, 67, 71, 85, 87, 90, 93, 95, 97, 99, 101, 103, 105, 109, 111, 113, 121, 125, 126, 131, 135, 137, 139, 141, 143, 145, 147, 149, 151, 153, 157, 165, 171, 173, 179, 181, 183, 187, 189; Will Heap 63, 158, 167, 177; David Loftus 155; David Munns 59; Sean Myers 61, 123; Lis Parsons 37, 39, 45, 56, 89, 115, 133, 169; William Reavell 81; Gareth Sambidge 83, 107; William Shaw 20, 41, 55, 129; Ian Wallace 25, 27, 49, 69, 73, 75, 77, 79, 117, 119, 175, 185.